NINETEENTH CENTURY HOME ARCHITECTURE

OF IOWA CITY

NINETEENTH CENTURY HOME ARCHITECTURE OF IOWA CITY

MARGARET N. KEYES

UNIVERSITY OF IOWA PRESS IOWA CITY

FOR MY PARENTS

CHARLES REUBEN KEYES AND SARAH NAUMANN KEYES

AND MY SISTER

CATHARINE KEYES MILLER

ACKNOWLEDGMENTS

Contributions to this publication, and to the research upon which it is based, deserve special recognition and an expression of appreciation. The author wishes to take this opportunity to acknowledge with genuine gratitude all who have contributed so much to both the investigation and this condensed report in book form.

Many individuals have given encouragement, inspiration, information, guidance, and supportive assistance to this work. The Graduate College, The University of Iowa, awarded a grant to finance this monograph; the State Historical Society of Iowa provided pertinent sources of information; and many Iowa City residents supplied previously undiscovered information.

Mr. Fred W. Kent made an invaluable contribution by providing many photographs which he had taken over the years, some as early as the 1910's. Other members of the University Photographic Service were untiring in efforts to supply additional photographs included.

The faculty committee at the Florida State University provided encouragement and guidance during the research period. Dr. Janet K. Smith was major professor in the formative stages; however, Dr. James E. Montgomery served in this capacity when the dissertation was completed.

Margaret N. Keyes
Iowa City, Iowa

June, 1967

CONTENTS

CHAPTER 1

INTRODUCTION

The home architecture of Iowa City represents many ethnic and cultural groups and is characteristic of all of the major architectural styles of the nineteenth century, the century of its development. In preparing this written and pictorial documentary record, the writer was compelled to develop an architectural classification as there is little agreement among architectural historians concerning terminology. Very few of the houses are "pure" examples of a specific style, but combine characteristics of two or more styles. However, sufficient characteristics of one style allow most of them to be classified as examples of that specific style.

Whenever possible, the date of construction of the houses has been given, except for those cases which lacked reliable sources. Johnson County and State of Iowa legal records, primarily deeds and real estate appraisement records (Data Sheets), were examined to aid in establishing accurate dates and to provide other pertinent information for the houses selected for the study. No nineteenth century tax records of the county have been located, and present county officers think that they probably were destroyed when the move to the present courthouse was made in 1900. Because the Data Sheets were recorded circa 1940, some of the dates for house construction may be inaccurate due to lack of information, lapse of memory of some of the residents, and, perhaps, guessing.

The bibliography included is the one used in the writer's doctoral dissertation with a few additions of recently found sources; however, it does not presume completeness for the broad field of nineteenth century home architecture. The names of the newspapers consulted vary considerably as owners and local conditions changed, but the citations given correspond to the listings in the files of the State Historical Society of Iowa, Iowa City.

CHAPTER 2

A BRIEF HISTORY OF IOWA CITY

THE FOUNDING OF IOWA CITY

Iowa City, home of the second and third capitals of the Territory of Iowa and of the first capital of the State of Iowa, was named before its location was determined. The First Legislative Assembly of the territory, meeting on January 1, 1839, at the Methodist Episcopal Church in Burlington, approved a bill to locate the permanent seat of government of the territory "at the most eligible point within the present limits of Johnson County."[1] On January 15, 1839, Colonel Thomas Cox, member of the assembly from Jackson County, made a motion to add the words, "to be called Iowa City,"[2] to the original bill and thus named the town before it was born. Governor Robert Lucas signed the bill into law on January 21, 1839.

Included in the bill was a provision for the appointment of three commissioners who would meet "on the first day of May, in the year eighteen hundred and thirty-nine, . . . at the town of Napoleon, and proceed to locate the Seat of Government . . ."[3] Elected to serve were Chauncey Swan, John Ronalds, and Robert Ralston. They met as directed at Napoleon (a town no longer in existence). In carrying out their assigned duties, the commissioners agreed that the principal requisites of the site for the new city were "health, beauty of location, good water, and convenience to timber and stone suitable for building."[4]

[1] *Journal of the House of Representatives of the First Legislative Assembly of Iowa Territory* (Burlington: Clarke and McKenny, Printers, 1839), pp. 162-163.
[2] *Ibid.*, p. 226.
[3] *Ibid.*, pp. 162-163.
[4] John B. Newhall, *Sketches of Iowa, or the Emigrant's Guide* (New York: J. H. Colton, 1841), p. 126.

On May 4, 1839, following several days of examining the land along the Iowa River above Napoleon, the commissioners officially located the new capital on the east bank of the river, about two miles north of Napoleon near the geographical center of Johnson County. The spot was marked by a post of wood placed about where "Old Capitol" now stands and which proclaimed the site as "Seat of Government, City of Iowa, May 4th, 1839" and signed "C. Swan, John Ronalds, Robt. Ralston, Commissioners."[5] All of the prerequisites had been fulfilled, "combined in an eminent degree, at the same spot, and centrally situated in the midst of a region of country which, for natural beauty and fertility of soil, may safely challenge a comparison with the world."[6]

Major John B. Newhall, native of Massachusetts and probably Iowa's most influential promoter in its formative years, described the availability of building materials as follows:

> Big Grove commences near Iowa City and extends to the borders of the Indian Territory. It has been pronounced among the best and most extensive bodies of timber in Iowa. It is situated between the Iowa and Cedar rivers, being about twenty miles in length with an average width of six to seven miles.
> Johnson County is abundantly supplied with excellent building rock, and its clay makes brick of the best quality. Perhaps few counties are more favored with all the requisites, either for the artisan or the agriculturist, than Johnson. . . .[7]

The local wood was mainly hickory and oak. Whatever pine lumber was used came to Iowa City by way of the Ohio and Mississippi rivers to Bloomington (early name for Muscatine), and from there it was transported inland.

SURVEYING THE SITE

Once the site for the new capital had been selected the duties of the original commission were complete and it was discharged. However, Chauncey Swan was appointed as Acting Commissioner of the new seat of government, and under his direction the survey for the town was begun in June, 1839, by Thomas Cox and John Frierson. By July 4, 1839, a draft of the first map of Iowa City was completed by Leander Judson who had been appointed to draw the plat. Illustration 1 is a copy of this first map.

The ground for Capitol Square was selected first by Commissioner Swan. From this starting point, streets, alleys, market places, church

---

[5] Charles Negus, "The Early History of Iowa," *Annals of Iowa*, Vol. 7, No. 4 (October, 1869), p. 326.

[6] Newhall, *op. cit.*, p. 126.

[7] *Ibid.*, p. 85.

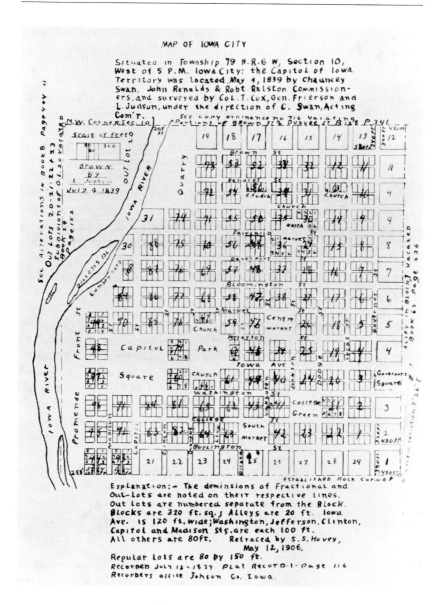

Illustration 1
Original Map of Iowa City (1839)
Courtesy, Fred W. Kent

sites, parks, a Governor's Square, and a Promenade along the Iowa River were surveyed and platted. All of the streets were named as shown in the illustration. Of these, all except Front Street are in use today.

To commemorate the completion of this original survey, a permanent stone column was erected at the southeast corner of the section at the corner of Outlot 1. It still stands at the corner of Summit and Court Streets, although its wording is almost completely obliterated by time and the action of the elements.

THE SALE OF TOWN LOTS

Following completion of the townsite surveys and recording of the map with Johnson County authorities, Governor Lucas proclaimed two public sales of lots, one in August, 1839, and the other the following October. The official notices, indicating that two hundred lots would be for sale, were circulated throughout the Territory and published in eastern newspapers as well. As the date of the August sale neared, the attractions of the new capital proved to be so great that a serious housing shortage developed since the town was without a hotel. Within a few days a double log cabin named "Lean-Back Hall" was constructed to accommodate the emigrant settlers who came to establish homes and the few eastern capitalists who planned to speculate in town lots. Tradition has it that thirty or more men shared the one bedroom, and the one bed, the floor.

Not only did "Lean-Back Hall" house the new arrivals and provide food and drink, but also it was the point of departure for the sale. With the auctioneer officiating from a horse-drawn wagon and the crowd following behind, the sale of lots began on North Clinton Street near the present location of the First Presbyterian Church. The sale continued for three days with one hundred and three lots being sold for a total sum of $17,292.75. The average lot price paid was $176.30, with the highest price paid for any one lot being $750 and the lowest $25.

The second sale of lots was held on the first Monday in October, 1839, the date proclaimed by the Governor. One hundred and six lots were purchased at this time. However, the total proceeds were somewhat less, $11,887, since the most desirable lots, those nearest Capitol Square, had been sold during the previous sale. The sale of lots from the original plat continued for several years.

THE EARLY CITY

Once lots had been purchased, the clearing of ground and the erection of homes and places of business began. At the time of the selection of the site as capital of the territory only one house was in existence, the log cabin of Matthew Teneick, who provided board for the three commissioners, according to Captain F. M. Irish who came to the area in 1839 and who also built his own log cabin. References in several early Iowa and Johnson County histories to the presence of log cabins in Iowa City serve to document this type of construction as that used in the earliest homes.

The growth of the frontier city was considered unparalleled by on-the-scene observers. One of them, Major Newhall, describes the new capital thus:

> . . . on the 4th of July, 1839, but one log cabin marked the place of a city. . . . On the following June after the elapse of eleven months, Iowa City contained between 6 and 700 inhabitants, several spacious hotels, a dozen stores, and artisans of every description, churches, coffee houses, and all the life and bustle of a city of years.[8]

> The unprecedented growth of Iowa City, from a wilderness frontier, beyond the pale of civilization, is indeed a wonder in the growth of towns . . . on the 1st day of May, 1839, this spot was the hunting-ground of the savage. . . . Up to the present time, 1840, being about fourteen months from the commencement of Iowa City, it contains a population of about 700 inhabitants . . . three or four brick buildings, and several others in progress, ten dry goods, grocery, and provision stores, one drug store, one saddlery, two blacksmiths, one gunsmith, three or four coffee houses, four lawyers, three physicians, one church, and one primary school. . . . I have heard of cities springing into existence as if by magic, but in no case have I ever known the application so just as when applied to this young capital of Iowa.[9]

According to another writer of the time, Nathan Howe Parker, Iowa City's population in 1840 was 520, and by 1845 it had doubled. Five years later it was 1,585, and in 1855 it was 5,000.

The report of H. H. Winchester, Esq., the precinct assessor, indicated that by mid-1844 the population had grown to a total of 916 with 186 families residing within the city. The rapid growth of the early town had subsided, as is usual with the beginnings of new capitals, but the foundations upon which Iowa City had developed remained firm as the editor of the *Standard* indicated:

> The present season there has been put under roof some half-a-dozen brick buildings of a superior class. . . . The erection of substantial dwellings, the completion of edifices already commenced . . . all indicate a steady advance.[10]

---

[8] *Ibid.*, pp. 84-85.
[9] *Ibid.*, pp. 125-129.
[10] Iowa *Standard*, September 12, 1844, p. 2.

An analysis of the places of birth of Iowa residents as recorded in the United States Census of 1860 revealed that the settlers coming from Ohio outnumbered those from Indiana, Pennsylvania, and New York by approximately two to one.[11]

Ohio	99,240
Indiana	57,555
Pennsylvania	52,156
New York	46,053
Illinois	26,696
New England States (6)	25,040

The total for the New England states, according to Petersen, is much less than would ordinarily be expected.[12]

An examination of the early membership rolls of the Johnson County Old Settlers' Organization shows that Ohio, Pennsylvania, and New York were the most frequently listed birthplaces of the members, while an analysis of the original nationalities of early Iowa City residents shows that, in addition to native-born Americans, the town was first settled by people from Ireland, Germany, and Scotland. Late in the 1840's a large number of new settlers arrived from Czecho-Slovakia. The newspapers of the early 1840's indicate that times were hard for the first settlers of Iowa City. Efforts to provide food, clothing, and shelter received top priority in the daily lives of the citizens. One newspaper editor wrote as follows in an editorial:

That our homes are, in general, small and inelegant, is true; but they are, nevertheless, in almost every case, sufficient for a good degree of comfort. Wood is abundant, and the huge fire places of the western cabins, when filled, will yield a degree of warmth that is capable of neutralizing the sturdiest attacks of Boreas.[13]

THE ESTABLISHMENT OF GOVERNMENT

Relocation of the Johnson County seat from Napoleon to Iowa City was authorized on December 18, 1839, by the Legislative Assembly. However, records in the files of the court of county commissioners dated October 7, 1839, indicate that the actual removal had taken place some two months earlier. They read as follows ". . . [We stand]

---

[11] *Eighth Census of the United States,* 1860, Population, p. 301, quoted in William J. Petersen, "Population Advance to the Upper Mississippi Valley, 1830-1860," *Iowa Journal of History and Politics,* Vol. 32, No. 3 (July, 1934), p. 320.

[12] Petersen, *op. cit.,* p. 334.

[13] Iowa *Standard,* April 27, 1843, p. 2.

adjourned to meet tomorrow morning at eight o'clock at the house of F. M. Irish in Iowa City."[14]

This "house" is presumed to be the log cabin to which Irish himself refers in his Johnson County history. The log cabin was later incorporated into a larger house and today forms the dining room of the Thomas S. Turner home (Illustrations 13 and 14). One corner of the original room showing the joining of the logs has been left unplastered and may be seen in the pantry adjoining the dining room.

The actual bringing of the seat of the territorial government to its intended site was not accomplished until 1842. Ground was broken for the Capitol building early in 1840, and work had progressed to the stage where the cornerstone was laid on July 4th of that year. This Greek Revival edifice, designed by John Francis Rague, has been described by Talbot Hamlin as "a simple but excellently designed building. . . ."[15] The Fifth Legislative Assembly, meeting on December 5, 1842, was the first to hold its sessions in the new capitol. It was the site of all assembly meetings until removal of the state capital to Des Moines in 1857. Today "Old Capitol" is the central administrative building of The University of Iowa.

From the early days of the Territorial Assembly statehood for Iowa had been the goal of its members. Finally, after many disappointments, on December 28, 1846, President James K. Polk signed the act of admission which proclaimed Iowa a State of the Union. Thus Iowa City became the first capital of the State of Iowa.

Residents of the state were deeply concerned with providing the best education possible for their young people. Public schools, a Female Academy, and a Mechanics Academy had been established within the city, but there was need for education at an advanced level. The First General Assembly of the new state, meeting in February, 1847, passed an act which provided for the State University of Iowa to be located at Iowa City. This was to be a most important factor in shaping the character of the future development of the city.

Until 1853, Iowa City was a city without its own government. True, it was the capital of the state and county seat of Johnson County, but it was not an incorporated town. Several attempts to do so had been made from 1841 on, but none of these was successful. Finally,

---

[14] Benjamin F. Shambaugh, *Iowa City: A Contribution to the Early History of Iowa.* (Iowa City: The State Historical Society of Iowa, 1893), p. 52.

[15] Talbot Hamlin, *Greek Revival Architecture in America* (London and New York: Oxford University Press, 1944), p. 255.

the state legislature proffered articles of incorporation to the inhabitants in 1853, and this time the citizens accepted the charter.

REMOVAL OF THE CAPITAL TO DES MOINES

The westward migration of the 1850's moved Iowa's center of population farther and farther away from the Mississippi River toward the Missouri. Because of the need to have the capital of the state centrally located, the Fifth General Assembly voted in January of 1855 to remove the seat of government from Iowa City to Des Moines. The same act transferred the capitol building to the University. The actual removal of the capital to Des Moines took place in the fall of 1857.

Thus, the shaping force of Iowa City after 1857 was The University of Iowa, which has made the city the recognized cultural and intellectual center of the state. Previously, the distinguishing characteristic had been political. Never has the city been an industrial center, although a few enterprises, such as a glove manufactory and a glass business, existed in the last half of the nineteenth century. Several industries have located there in the twentieth century, but the University continues to influence all facets of community life.

CHAPTER 3

ARCHITECTURAL STYLES OF NINETEENTH CENTURY HOUSES IN IOWA CITY

THE EARLIEST HOUSES

The log cabin apparently was the earliest method of construction used in Iowa City houses, hotels, and places of business. According to Harold R. Shurtleff, the log cabin type of construction was not commonly used in the New England or Southern colonies in the seventeenth century but was first introduced in Delaware about 1640 by settlers from Sweden.[1] As the country expanded westward in the eighteenth and nineteenth centuries and land clearing made logs readily available for construction, the method was frequently used in the newly established territories.

An early Iowa City log cabin was discovered in August of 1926 when a house at 514 North Gilbert Street belonging to Mr. John Lechty was being demolished. According to Mr. Fred W. Kent, who photographed the cabin (Illustration 2), and Mr. Gordon Kent, who also viewed the structure, no one, not even the owners of the house, was aware that the house being razed had been constructed around a log cabin. Such practice was common many years ago, according to older residents of the city. The log cabin was described as "a one-room affair, built up of roughly hewn logs mortised together at the corners and the cracks filled with mortar. . . ."[2] Old settlers still living in 1926

---

[1] Harold R. Shurtleff, *The Log Cabin Myth* (Cambridge: Harvard University Press, 1939), p. 3.
[2] Iowa City *Press-Citizen*, August 13, 1926, p. 2.

Illustration 2
Early Iowa City Log Cabin (Non-Extant)
Photographed August 18, 1926
Courtesy, Fred W. Kent

recollected that the structure "was constructed in 1839 or 1840."[3] The cabin presented a picture of characteristics typical of such a building except for the interior position of the chimney and the smooth framing boards around the entrance and the windows. These framing boards no doubt had replaced the original frames when the new house was added to the cabin. The original deed to this property, dated February 13, 1849, was from the State of Iowa to Thomas Hughs [Hughes?], according to the *Abstract of Original Deeds from the State of Iowa, for Lots in Iowa City* (manuscript in the Johnson County Courthouse, Iowa City). Presumably, because of the date of the deed, the log cabin was constructed for or by Hughs or for someone who had "squatter's rights" before him.

Captain Irish recorded that "the first regularly built house was erected by Mr. Teneick [Teneyck?], on the corner of Iowa Avenue and Dubuque Street." This was the same gentleman who occupied the first

[3] Iowa City *Press-Citizen*, August 14, 1926, p. 2.

house in Iowa City, a log cabin. Teneick's second home was "of solid hewn lumber, quite roomy and two stories high." After serving as a residence, a tavern, and a boarding house for over twenty years, the house was destroyed by fire.[4]

Apparently, clapboard construction was popular for the building of subsequent early houses. Irish described them as follows:

> . . . a large number of buildings were in process of erection, displaying every variety of architecture, from the most rudely constructed log cabin to the well-finished two-story frame house. Mr. Henry Felkner had erected a saw mill (the first in the county) . . . but this mill could supply but a small portion of the demand for lumber, and many of the first houses built in the city were sided up with clapboards split from trunks of large white or burr oak trees. These boards were from four to six feet in length and from six to eight inches in width, and split as thin as the timber would admit of. They were then smoothed upon one side with a drawing knife, shaved down to nearly an equal thickness, and after this preparation, they constituted a weather boarding, answering a very good purpose, and in many instances lasting for twenty years.[5]

No further comments concerning "every variety of architecture" in the above quotation were made by Captain Irish, and no other early writers of Iowa City history refer to architectural styles. Apparently, none of the early frame dwellings built of clapboards remains standing today. At the time Irish wrote his history (1868) probably none was still extant since he stated that many lasted only "for twenty years."

The first bricks to be made in Iowa City were handcrafted in April of 1840 by Sylvanus Johnson who later in 1857 built his own home of brick on the north edge of Iowa City (the Johnson-Bodine-Lang house, Illustration 61). William Bostick [Bostwick?] was the owner of the first brick house in Iowa City, constructed by George T. Andrews, a mason, of bricks from Johnson's kiln.[6] Two lots of Block 79, which is located at the northeast corner of Iowa Avenue and Clinton Street, were originally owned by Bostick, according to the *Abstract of Original Deeds.* Which lot was the site of the brick house is not known since it was demolished many years ago. The area encompassing both lots is now the location of the College of Business Administration, The University of Iowa. Irish described the house as a modest one-story structure. No other reference to this house has been found except in later histories which quote Irish.

---

[4] F. [Frederick] M. Irish, "History of Johnson County, Iowa," *Annals of Iowa,* Vol. 6, No. 1 (January 1868), p. 29.

[5] *Ibid.,* p. 110.

[6] *Ibid.*

The use of local stone for construction was not discussed by Captain Irish; however, its availability had been considered of prime importance by the city's founders.

HOUSES WITH COLONIAL CHARACTERISTICS

Although the early homes of the nineteenth century in Iowa City were constructed at the time when the Greek Revival style was dominant in the country, many of these homes show pronounced characteristics of the Colonial style. These include the gable roof with a central chimney or chimneys at both ends, the central doorway flanked by one or two windows, floor plans featuring a central hall with one or two rooms on either side, windows with small panes of glass, and the New England salt-box house form with a lean-to at the rear. Familiarity with the Colonial style and substyles as well as sentimental attachment to former homes probably explains the presence of such characteristics. Houses in Iowa City which illustrate this influence were constructed of brick and stone, either limestone or sandstone.

THE HUTCHINSON-KUHL HOUSE

Perhaps the earliest house still standing in Iowa City is the limestone home of Professor and Mrs. E. P. Kuhl (Illustrations 3 and 4) on the west side of the Iowa River. It may well be contemporary with the previously mentioned Irish and Hughs-Lechty log cabins and presumably was constructed "before or about 1840." A former early Iowa City resident who lived in the neighborhood when the Kuhls purchased the house in April of 1927 told the new owners that he recalled working for the farmer who owned the house "in the early 1840's."[7] Who this farmer was has not been established, but Johnson County records show that the first owner of the property was Robert Hutchinson. Since the date of the deed transferring the property from the Territory of Iowa to Hutchinson is March 16, 1843, the assumption is made that the house was originally built for or by Hutchinson while he held a claim to the property. The records of the Johnson County Claim Association indicate that he had settled on the property before the land was sold by the government and that, at the time of the sale, he was the one person allowed to bid on it.[8]

---

[7] Interview, Professor and Mrs. E. P. Kuhl, March 26, 1965.

[8] Charles [Clarence] Ray Aurner, *Leading Events in Johnson County, Iowa, History,* Vol. 1, Historical (Cedar Rapids, Iowa: Western Historical Press, 1912), pp. 402-403.

Illustration 3
The Hutchinson-Kuhl House
119 Park Road
Photographed May 1927
Courtesy, Fred W. Kent

Illustration 4
The Hutchinson-Kuhl House (as remodeled)

Originally, the structure was a farmhouse outside the city limits, but today it is well within those boundaries. The limestone used in the random ashlar construction of the house is the same as that employed in the base and lower part of "Old Capitol" and probably came from a no-longer-active quarry located a few blocks north of the Kuhl residence.

During the construction of "Old Capitol" a new source of building rock, a sandstone, was discovered that was considered superior in quality to the limestone.[9] Information given to the Kuhls by the late Benjamin F. Shambaugh, director of the State Historical Society of Iowa, who studied Iowa City history extensively, indicates that the rejected limestone was used in the construction of their home. The walls are about twenty-six inches at their greatest width in the basement and are approximately eighteen to twenty inches at the first floor window sills.

Comparison of photographs of the house as it was in 1927 when purchased by the Kuhls and as it stands today shows several alterations, each of which enhances the overall Colonial character of the house. These include removal of the front porch which no doubt was an addition to the original house, installation of windowpanes containing six lights per sash as original windows found in the basement indicated, raising the roof six feet at the point of the gable to allow for rooms on the second floor, cutting into the roof three dormers on the front of the house and one long dormer on the rear, and replacing the simple undecorated cornice with one featuring dentils and cornice returns at the ends.

Apparently, the original house was heated by iron stoves in each room, for there were no fireplaces. In the remodeling a new exterior chimney was built, using only the original stone, thus creating a fireplace in the new enlarged living room which combined two smaller rooms at the left of the entrance. The central entrance hallway was extended through the house to the back door, and stairs were added to the second floor which had been an unfinished loft. Openings for a second window and a door were made in the west end of the house which previously had only one window, probably in keeping with the early practice of using as few openings as possible on the side of the prevailing winds. All of the interior door and window moldings are the original ones.

The overall appearance of the house is Colonial rather than a later

---

[9] Iowa City *Standard,* March 12, 1842, p. 2.

style. The observer is reminded of the appearance of several of the more modest homes in the Colonial Williamsburg restoration.

THE BARNES-CROWLEY AND ARN-WARREN HOUSES

Two modest one-story houses, both constructed of native yellow-brown sandstone and laid in the random ashlar technique, show much similarity and are predominantly Colonial in style. They are the Barnes-Crowley house (Illustration 5) and the Arn-Warren house, which was razed in the spring of 1966 (Illustration 6). The *Abstract of Original Deeds* shows that the original owner of the former property was Almon Barnes, who received the deed from the Territory of Iowa on May 29, 1846. The first owner of the latter house, according to the *Johnson County Transfer Book, Iowa City & Additions, No. 1*, was Michael Arn. This is confirmed by Mrs. Walter C. Chudwick, Iowa City, who is a granddaughter of Arn. Although no exact construction date is available for either house, their simplicity and honesty of construction and their lack of decorative detail, as well as comparison with houses known to have been constructed in the 1840's, indicate that they were built in the decade between 1840 and 1850.

Both houses have the formal Colonial orientation of facade with one window on either side of the doorway. The doorway of the Arn-Warren house was centered, but that of the Barnes-Crowley house is placed slightly to the right of center. Since the latter house has a central chimney as in early Colonial days, the off-center entrance was no doubt a device to accommodate this feature in the floor plan. An earlier picture of the Arn-Warren house showed chimneys at either end of the gable.[10] The doorway of each house has a recessed transom of three rectangular lights above it, a frequently-used Colonial device. Whereas the Barnes-Crowley house has windows irregularly placed in each end of the house, the Arn-Warren house had only one small window in each end. Each was placed high in the gable and toward the front of the house to allow for the chimney stack. The sash windows of the Arn-Warren house had two panes of glass in each sash. The windows of the Barnes-Crowley house employ one pane of glass per sash, but these apparently are not the original window style since on the north side there is one window which has six small panes of glass per sash.

---

[10] Edwin Charles Ellis, "Certain Stylistic Trends in Architecture in Iowa City" (unpublished master's thesis, State University of Iowa, 1947), p. 50.

Illustration 5
The Barnes-Crowley House
614 North Johnson Street

Illustration 6
The Arn-Warren House (Non-Extant)
730 South Dubuque Street

The Barnes-Crowley house has lintels and sills of blocks of dressed stone which project rather sharply from the house, while the only suggestion of lintels in the Arn-Warren house was the placing of longer-than-usual rectangular blocks of sandstone over the openings. These were a part of the random ashlar treatment and thus were not smoothed to contrast with the background.

THE NICKING AND ALBRIGHT-ZION-LUTHERAN HOUSES

A second pair of early sandstone houses reflects knowledge of the New England Colonial salt-box style. The house last owned by the Zion Lutheran Church and torn down in August of 1965 (Illustration 7) was a one-story example of the style, and the Henry C. Nicking house (Illustration 8) is a story-and-a-half interpretation of the style. Today the old Nicking house, long considered an Iowa City landmark, houses two business enterprises.

The *Abstract of Original Deeds* shows that the first owner of the property on which the one-story house stood was Henry Albright, who received the deed from the state on September 6, 1847. Although he was not the original owner of the property at 410 East Market Street, Henry C. Nicking apparently built the house which stands there. The late Miss Louise Reiss, granddaughter of Nicking, was quoted in a newspaper article as saying that the house was constructed by her grandfather in 1854 and that the contractors were Finkbine and Loveless [Lovelace?].[11]

The one-story ells on the rear of both houses were constructed of brick and stone, and both appear to have been a part of the original structure. In the case of the Nicking house, the ell has been reinforced and covered by concrete.

Except for the row of half-windows in the half-story of the Nicking house, the facades were identical in organization with two windows on either side of the central entrance. The Nicking house has shutters at the windows, and, since an earlier picture of the house includes them, they are not a recent addition but probably were a part of the nineteenth century architectural design. The Nicking house has no windows in either the east or west ends, although there is evidence that a small one in the point of the east gable has been closed. In the Albright house there was a single window in each end toward the rear of the main block of the house and behind the chimney stack.

---

[11] Mabel Tompkins, "City's Oldest [sic] House Still Stems Modernization Trend," *The Daily Iowan* [n.d., unpaged].

Illustration 7
The Albright-Zion Lutheran House (Non-Extant)
613 East Davenport Street

Illustration 8
The Nicking House
410 East Market Street

Both houses had interior chimney stacks at either end of a gable roof.

THE WINDREM-GREEN HOUSE

The two-story limestone and brick home of Edwin B. Green (Illustration 9) probably was constructed by William Windrem. Deed records of Johnson County show that Windrem purchased the property from the Territory of Iowa on November 17, 1845. Windrem, born in 1801 in Ireland, came to America in 1830 where he learned the carpenter's trade in Ogdensburg, New York. From there he came to Iowa City in 1842 and was employed as a carpenter on the capitol building then under construction. Windrem "continued his trade for several years and assisted with the erection of many pioneer buildings, all prior to 1850."[12] Because of the general architectural character of the house and the foregoing quotation, the assumption is made that the house was built by Windrem after 1845 and before 1850. The remodeling of the house was begun in the early 1940's by the late Miss Merle Ford and completed by the present owner.

Older residents of Iowa City have reported many times that this house was a stagecoach stop. Evidence in support of this statement has not been found. However, one source provides information which states that a stagecoach company was located within the same block as the house:

On block twenty-five, which is bounded by Jefferson, Dodge, and Iowa Avenue, and Johnson Street, the [Western Stage] company began the construction of stables, with Finkbine and Lovelace as contractors, and here manufactured all the required articles in use by the concern; coaches, harness, and minor articles were made on the ground.[13]

The transfers of deeds of the house property do not indicate that the stagecoach company or its manager, W. H. McChesney, owned it, but an 1895 picture of the house owned by Mr. Green shows extensive barns and stables behind the house.

Outstanding Colonial characteristics of the house include the arrangement of the facade openings; the use of unequal lights in the windows, nine in the upper sashes and six in the lower ones; the narrow flat cornice with short returns; chimneys with molded brick caps at

---

[12] Charles [Clarence] Ray Aurner, *Leading Events in Johnson County, Iowa, History*, Vol. 2, Biographical (Cedar Rapids: Western Historical Press, 1913), pp. 839-840. This information was supplied by James H. Windrem, son of William Windrem.

[13] Aurner, Vol. 1, *op. cit.*, p. 206.

Illustration 9
The Windrem-Green House
604 Iowa Avenue

either end of the gable roof; and the floor plan with a central hallway extending through the house.
The second-floor windows have wood lintels which are the original
ones. In place of such treatment on the first floor, long blocks of
quarried limestone were placed over the windows and the doorway,
much in the same manner as was used in the Arn-Warren house. Today these lintels have been replaced with concrete. Most of the windowpanes are the original ones.
In the 1895 picture there was a square wood porch which extended
across the area between the two interior windows. A balcony was
located above the porch and was supported by narrow square piers
and had a protective railing. In the remodeling this feature was replaced with the present balcony. The balusters are turned wood, and
four scrolled brackets of wood give visual support to the structure.
The first-floor plan utilizes a narrow central hall with two rooms on
either side, a study and a furnace room to the left, and the dining
room and the kitchen to the right. On the second floor there is a
large living room on the west side and two bedrooms on the east.
Originally, each floor had four rooms. In the remodeling the staircase

which had extended from the front of the house to the back was reversed.

THE WELCH-TROTT HOUSE

Essentially composed of Colonial characteristics, although the entrance is at one side of the facade, the house on North Van Buren Street owned by Emil G. Trott (Illustration 10) has a feature commonly seen in houses of Flemish and Dutch Colonial style. This is the extension of the brick end walls above the roof line and incorporating the chinmeys. The gable pitch is straight-lined and concludes with an "elbow" or a step at the corners. Across the front of the house below the wood cornice is a decorative brick frieze with the headers forming a dentil pattern which suggests an attempt to produce a classic entablature in a modest house. An outline of a framing with pilasters shows around the front door. Probably, this was an addition to the original house since the present door and windows all have flat stone lintels. The foundation is of rubble limestone above which is a water table of dressed stone on the facade.

County records indicate that the house was built for Maria F. Welch in 1875, although the overall character of the house suggests that the date may have been somewhat earlier.

Illustration 10
The Welch-Trott House
630 North Van Buren Street

THE TEMPLIN-FENLON AND JOHNSON-WILSON HOUSES

Several brick houses, laid in common bond, modest in style, and of one-story or one-and-one-half-story type, are also essentially Colonial in overall character. Of these, the Templin-Fenlon house (Illustration 11) and the Johnson-Wilson house (Illustration 12) show characteristics which combine the Colonial and the Georgian style which followed.

Illustration 11
The Templin-Fenlon House
729 East Market Street

Illustration 12
The Johnson-Wilson House
412 North Dubuque Street

Segmental arched headings, an Early Georgian characteristic, appear above the facade windows in both houses and over the Johnson-Wilson doorway. However, the windows and door retain the usual rectangular shape with framing filling in the curved portion of the low arch. Curved lintels formed by bricks placed in a vertical position are used in both houses. Those in the Johnson-Wilson house become more decorative by a heightened projection in the center of the lintel which suggests the keystone form. Both houses have window sills of dressed stone, with those in the Templin-Fenlon house resting on a support of two protruding bricks at either side.

Flanking the doorway of the Templin-Fenlon house are fluted pilasters with decorative Corinthian capitals which support a broad classic cornice. This treatment is Georgian in character. Above the cornice appears the same brick segmental heading as seen over the windows, suggesting that the decorative door treatment was an addition to the original home.

Horizontal boarding was used to finish the end walls in the upper part of the gable peak of the Templin-Fenlon house. A third material, limestone, laid in the rubble manner, forms the foundation of the house which extends above ground level and raises the first floor three steps above the ground.

Two iron stars appear on each end of the Templin-Fenlon house at the second-floor level. These are the terminals of reinforcing tie rods which extend from one end of the house to the other. Such devices are often seen on many older Iowa City houses.

No information concerning building dates of either house was found. James D. Templin, the original owner of the East Market Street property, was granted the title by the Territory of Iowa on May 31, 1846, according to the *Abstract of Original Deeds*. He was also the first owner of several other properties, and no information is available which indicates where he located his own home or whether he built this house or not. Sylvanus Johnson, the first brick-maker, was the first owner of the Dubuque Street property, obtaining it from the state on March 16, 1847. Because he was the only brickmaker in Iowa City prior to 1856, the assumption is made that he supplied the brick for the house and perhaps built it for himself.

Other houses which show characteristics of the Colonial styles include the Frank D. Person duplex, 321-323 East Davenport Street, the Frances C. Dalton house, 613 North Gilbert Street, and the Evelyn L. Bickett house, 332 South Governor Street. The latter house was discovered to be constructed of sandstone in very recent years when the siding which covered it was removed.

HOUSES OF THE GREEK REVIVAL STYLE

Popular from about 1820 to 1860, the Greek Revival style varied from region to region within the United States, and the Midwestern interpretations are in general simpler and less likely to follow the temple style than their prototypes in the eastern and southern parts of the country. The local culture, as well as the materials available for construction and the climate of the areas, affected the architecture of the style, according to Talbot Hamlin, author of *Greek Revival Architecture in America*. Several sources indicate that Greek Revival houses in the Midwest employed typical two-to-three basic proportions, were frequently built of clapboard, were less ornamented than houses of the style in the East and South, and often were one-story structures. Their roofs usually had a low pitch, the gable end frequently faced the street, chimneys were inconspicuous, and lintels and cornices were plain. Jigsaw brackets under the eaves, a decorative motif of the Victorian period, began to be seen after 1840, and round pillars were replaced by thin, square posts. Throughout the Midwestern agricultural area houses very much like the classic revival ones in Ohio and the East were being built with native materials and limited, often crude, workmanship. Frank J. Roos, Jr., found that stone was used in Ohio as the material of construction for many of the larger houses of classic influence.[14]

The Greek Revival style in Iowa City houses has many of the characteristics of the style as it was expressed in Ohio, Indiana, and other Midwestern areas. The use of native materials, stone for example, is seen; many are simple in concept, suggesting Colonial ancestry; and the full portico style is seen in only two instances. No record has been found which indicates that there were other porticoed houses, but some probably were built which are no longer in existence.

---

[14] Wilbur D. Peat, *Indiana Houses of the Nineteenth Century* (Indianapolis: Indiana Historical Society, 1962), pp. 37-51; Henry Lionel Williams and Ottalie K. Williams, *A Guide to Old American Houses* (New York: A. S. Barnes and Company, 1962), pp. 82-114; Hamlin, *op. cit.*, p. vii, pp. 210 and 283; Frank J. Roos, Jr., "An Investigation of the Sources of Early Architectural Design in Ohio," (unpublished doctoral dissertation, Ohio State University, 1937), p. 91.

Houses With Porticoes

THE IRISH-HAMILTON-TURNER HOUSE

The Irish-Hamilton-Turner house (Illustrations 13 and 14) is the only extant nineteenth century Iowa City house with a full double portico. It also has a one-story portico on two sides of the east wing of the house.

Captain F. M. Irish was the original owner of this property, and the log cabin which he built upon it was probably the first home called "Rose Hill" by the Irish family. The present house was constructed around the cabin, and today that early structure forms the dining room. Hamlin indicated that it was not unusual to cover earlier log buildings with clapboarding and to add dormers and classic porches.[15] The date for the construction of the present house is not known. However, a newspaper article indicates that such a structure was planned in 1860:

Wm. Hamilton, Esq., a former citizen of this place, and lately of Linn Co., has purchased that part of the Rose Hill property, comprised in the old homes[t]ead of Capt. Irish and proposes to build upon that lovely eminence what will be by far the finest residence in the county, if but half as elegant as his house at Mt. Vernon.[16]

Legal records show that William Hamilton purchased the property on October 1, 1860, and held it until July 29, 1865. Real estate appraisement data give 1870 for the present house, with 1840 as the date for the log cabin part.[17]

Other owners of the property who played significant roles in community life were George E. Kimball, who operated the "Rose Hill Nursery" in the 1870's, and David Borts, a contractor-builder.

An early illustration of the house (Illustration 13) shows it much as it stands today except for a mansard roof, a cupola, the position of the chimneys, and a balustrade on the roof of the one story portico. Whether or not the French roof was the original one is not known. A 1913 picture in Aurner's *Leading Events in Johnson County, Iowa, History*, Vol. 2, shows the present hipped roof.

The double portico supports the hip roof and is composed of four square wood columns, Doric in style, with a balcony at the second-floor level. The railing, composed mainly of circular forms, is carved

---

[15] Hamlin, *op. cit.*

[16] Iowa City *State Press*, October 16, 1860, p. 3.

[17] *Data Sheets, Real Estate Appraisement*, Ward 3, p. 472. Hereafter called *Data Sheets*.

Illustration 13
The Irish-Hamilton-Turner House
(Lithograph drawing from *Johnson County, Iowa, Atlas,* 1870, page 28.)

Illustration 14
The Irish-Hamilton-Turner House
1310 Cedar Street

from wood. The entablature board under the cornice is broad and undecorated.

The south facade is arranged asymmetrically with the entrance placed at the right and two windows to the left. The second-floor openings are identically placed. The original sash windows were composed of small panes, several of which still remain on the rear of the house. Each window has a narrow flat lintel and louvered shutters.

The front entrance has a paneled door, two narrow vertical lights on either side, and a broad, classic cornice that projects sharply from the siding. Four pilasters that repeat the square form of the columns give visual support to this cornice. The doorway opens into a small hallway from which a graceful staircase with a railing of native black walnut curves upward to the second floor. To the left of the hall is the living room and behind it a study. Two fireplaces, placed back to back, are on the wall which separates the two rooms. Behind the entrance hall and to its right is the original log cabin which is now the dining room. This room also has a fireplace. The extension to the right of the log cabin area is a large kitchen; adjoining it is the pantry. Upstairs there are four bedrooms. The interior moldings, thought to be the original ones, are rounded and classic in character.

THE DOWNEY-PICKERING-GLASGOW HOUSE

"Prospect Hill," the early home of Hugh D. Downey, attorney, banker, real estate dealer, and a member of the first Board of Trustees of the State University, and now belonging to Mr. and Mrs. Bruce R. Glasgow (Illustrations 15 and 16), is a one-story example of the Greek Revival style with a pedimented portico. Located high on a hill in the north part of the original town, the house is said to have been designed by John F. Rague, architect of "Old Capitol." No information has been found which verifies this.

Some confusion exists concerning the first owner of the property and the possible date of construction. According to the *Abstract of Original Deeds,* Outlot 15 on which the house stands was originally deeded to John H. Lyons on November 13, 1856. However, the 1854 Millar map of Iowa City not only locates the house accurately but also pictures it and identifies the owner as Downey. He is listed as an owner of the property in the *Johnson County Transfer Book,* but the date of his deed is not given.

Another occupant of the house was John A. A. Pickering, who operated a china, glass, and gift store.

Illustration 15
The Downey-Pickering-Glasgow House
(Lithograph drawing from Millar Map of Iowa City, 1854)

Illustration 16
The Downey-Pickering-Glasgow House (before remodeling)
834 North Johnson Street
Photograph not dated
Courtesy, Mr. and Mrs. Bruce R. Glasgow

The present owners of the house date it circa 1844 because of information from the late William R. Hart, Iowa City attorney and historian. Ellis in his thesis gave 1840-1842 dates for the house, apparently from information he obtained from a former owner, Professor Mary Holmes, formerly of The University of Iowa's Art Department, but he did not document the source.[18] Conflicting data in the real estate appraisement sheets date the house as 1870. The accuracy of the drawing of the house on the 1854 map would tend to support neither date and probably indicates that the house was built prior to the date of the map.

The portico extends across the central two-thirds of the south facade and features four fluted Doric columns under a complete entablature. Over the central part of this cornice is a shallow pediment with flush boarding in the tympanum. The floor plan of the house is in the shape of a Latin cross with the head of the cross projecting onto the portico. This projection is about the width of the pediment. Entrance from the porch was centered in the projection and was directly into the front parlor. In the present remodeling this entrance has been replaced by a window and the front of the house is now on the left side. The house was built on a limestone foundation, and the exterior treatment of the projecting area was done with flush boarding with the remainder of the original house having overlapping clapboards.

The interior has been extensively remodeled because of the deteriorated condition of the house when the Glasgows purchased it, and apparently, the house had undergone previous remodelings. The original shape of the house has been maintained insofar as it could be determined, but the arrangement of rooms has been altered considerably. Originally, the floor plan accommodated two parlors and four smaller rooms, probably bedrooms, in the horizontal bar or arms of the cross. Behind the front parlor was a back parlor with two smaller rooms on either side. The long part of the vertical bar, or the body of the cross, was composed of the dining, kitchen, and service areas. The house had no hallways. On either side of the long bar were porches which had Doric columns.

Evidence of formal landscaping of the house still remains. The long approach to the house from Brown Street had a row of trees on either side, some of which are still living. The house was set above several terraces, the topmost of which was of brick with a low stone retaining wall. Much of this original terrace is still in place.

---

[18] Ellis, *op. cit.*, p. 56.

Houses Without Porticoes

Three extant houses represent a vernacular interpretation of the Greek Revival style, each without porticoes and each with the entrance in the gable end of the house. A fourth, which has been razed, was architecturally and historically significant and similar in style.

THE GOVERNOR ROBERT LUCAS HOUSE

"Plum Grove" (Illustration 17), Governor Lucas' home in the southeast part of the city, was restored in 1946, Iowa's centennial year, by the Iowa State Conservation Commission. The house was constructed in the fall of 1844 after Iowa's first Territorial governor moved his family back to Iowa following a short sojourn in their native Ohio. Lucas and his wife, Friendly, patterned the house somewhat after their Piketon, Ohio, home. The brick work is laid in common bond with every eighth row composed of headers. Since Sylvanus Johnson

Illustration 17
The Governor Lucas House
727 Switzer Avenue

was the only brickmaker in the city prior to 1856 when Nicholas Oakes set up his kiln, the assumption is made that Johnson provided the bricks for "Plum Grove."

Facing north, the house has an asymmetrically-arranged facade with the entrance at the left side. Over the simply paneled door is a transom of four square lights. The gable area produces the effect of a pediment due to the cornice returns. The entablature board is narrower than those seen in many houses of this style and is void of decoration. In the tympanum of the gable is a round window with eight triangularly shaped panes. The brick work around this window is circular in treatment. Over the doorway and the windows, bricks are laid vertically to form lintels. All windows have louvered shutters. The house has four chimneys, two on the west side, one on the east, and one on the ell. Those in the main block of the house serve a fireplace on each floor.

The house is square in plan with a square kitchen ell at the rear. The narrow entrance hall has a curving staircase. Other rooms on the first floor are a parlor, a study (probably these were "front" and "rear" parlors in the nineteenth century), a dining room, and a buttery opening from the kitchen. Upstairs are three bedrooms. All of the interior woodwork is of native black walnut which was cut from the site; this includes the staircase, the fireplaces, and the window and door framings. The floors are of white oak planks.

A two-story ell on the west and south sides and a porch across the north and west had been added to the house during the years, and all but one of the fireplaces had been either plastered over, bricked in, or removed. In the restoration these additions were removed, and the rooms were returned to their original plan. A new staircase was built because of the bad condition of the old one, but the curved railing is the original.

THE GILMAN FOLSOM HOUSE

The Gilman Folsom house (Illustration 18) was located on the bluff on the west side of the Iowa River where "Westlawn," which houses administrative offices of the University's College of Nursing, now stands. Aurner recorded that "this old brick house was built in 1851 and the material in the main portion came from the kilns of Sylvanus Johnson. . . ."[19] Folsom was a lawyer.

This house, which was similar to "Plum Grove" but seemingly more

---

[19] Aurner, Vol. 1, *op. cit.*, p. 626.

Illustration 18
The Folsom House (Non-Extant) Photographed February 1923
Courtesy, Fred W. Kent

of a mansion, had the cornice and broad entablature carried completely across the gable end. There was no opening in the tympanum. The entrance was at the right side; the door was paneled and had a transom of six panes with three vertical lights on either side. Fluted pilasters separated the side lights and the door. The door and all of the windows in the gable end had lintels of dressed stone. Other windows had lintels of vertical bricks.

Apparently, four chimneys serviced the main block of the house. Two others served the wings.

No information was located concerning the plan of the house. However, the location of the chimneys and the entrance suggests that it was a reverse plan of "Plum Grove."

The Gilman Folsom Collection of the State Historical Society of Iowa contains several items of interest concerning the home. One is a receipt for payment on April 14, 1851, of the following items: "25 brick for Hearth and jambs, $.20; 1½ days' work by E. White, @ $2.50,

$3.75; Laying Hearth and joints, $1.50; Work on kitchen, $10.50."[20] Another, dated August 8, 1852, by E. C. Cole, includes: "Painting 24 frames, $3.00; Priming cornice, $1.50; One half day's work, $.75; Painting cornice, $1.50."[21]

An insurance policy issued by the Aetna Insurance Company, Hartford, Connecticut, and dated December 20, 1862, carries this description:

> . . . Three Thousand Dollars on his Brick Dwelling house—main part 2 story with a one story wing on the west—occupied by the assured & situated on the west side of the Iowa River & a few rods west of Iowa City, Iowa.
> Four Hundred Dollars on his Rosewood Piano & Six Hundred Dollars on his household furniture—said Furniture & Piano being contained in the above described dwelling. . . .[22]

Another insurance policy dated December 21, 1868, includes this statement: "Permission is hereby granted to use Kerosene for Light."[23]

THE BRANCH-LINDER HOUSE

The Henry Linder house (Illustration 19) was built in 1852. Therefore, the original owner must have been S. F. W. Branch, who is listed as the only owner of the property before 1866.

This house today represents a transitional style wherein the coming Gothic Revival is heralded by the decorative hood over the entrance in the gable end and the elongated arch-like brackets at the top of the square columns on the side porch. The house has a large wing to the left of the main block which was an addition, probably about 1875. There is no cornice return emphasizing the pediment. All other characteristics are similar to the two houses of the style previously discussed. The decorative railing around the front steps was added by the Linders when they restored the house.

THE STRUP-KURZ HOUSE

Also showing decorative details of later styles is the Strup-Kurz house (Illustration 20). The house has decorative coupled brackets with pendants under the broad overhang of the gable, and the cornice is barely discernible. The window cornices and entablatures, however, are deeply projecting and in accord with characteristics of the classic style.

---

[20] The Gilman Folsom Collection, State Historical Society of Iowa, Iowa City, Iowa. Manuscript.

[21] *Ibid.*

[22] *Ibid.*

[23] *Ibid.*

Illustration 19
The Branch-Linder House
120 North Dodge Street

Illustration 20
The Strup-Kurz House
309 East Church Street

County records show 1885 as the year in which this house was constructed, but because of its overall character this date is open to question.

The Starr-Startsman-Ritter house, 110 East Bloomington Street, and the Rothweiler-Fountain house, 310 North Gilbert Street, also illustrate Greek Revival houses with entrances in the gable end.

A group of six houses illustrates another local interpretation of the Greek Revival style. Each has the entrance centered in the side parallel to the ridgepole of the gable roof. Two are of native sandstone, two of brick, and two are clapboarded.

THE WENTZ-SCHROCK AND THE WENTZ-STACH HOUSES

Two random ashlar, yellow-brown sandstone houses provide simple, chaste examples of the Greek Revival style in the Midwest. They are the Wentz-Schrock house (Illustration 21) which was torn down in May, 1966, and the Wentz-Stach house (Illustration 22).

Jacob Wentz, a native of Germany, purchased the Market Street property on June 28, 1847, and is considered to have begun construction of the house in that year. Of interest is the fact that Caroline Wentz received the deed to the Gilbert Street site on the same date in 1847.[24] The relationship of these two persons is not known; however, if they were not man and wife, they probably were related. Because of the similarity of style and material and also because of the location and ownership, the two houses were probably built about the same time. The use of brackets under the eaves of the Stach house suggests that it may have been built a few years later. The Wentz-Stach house is a larger, more elaborate structure than the Wentz-Schrock house. The doorway treatment, the larger scale of the house, the large clapboard "lean-to" at the rear, the use of four chimney stacks, the more decorative cornice board, all indicate that the Gilbert Street house was more of a mansion than the Market Street one.

Both houses had broad cornices across the facade. The Schrock house had a short cornice return, but on the Stach house only the eaves form a brief return. The Schrock house was raised five steps above the ground, suggesting the Georgian device to make a house seem prepossessing. The Stach house is placed only two steps above the ground.

---

[24] *Abstract of Original Deeds,* pp. 13 and 17.

Illustration 21
The Wentz-Schrock House (Non-Extant)
409 East Market Street

Illustration 22
The Wentz-Stach House
219 North Gilbert Street

THE F. M. IRISH AND THE LOUISE B. KELLY HOUSES

The house owned by Mrs. Louise B. Kelly on Reno Street (Illustration 23) is located on property which abuts the original Irish land on the west, and it and the home of Captain F. M. Irish (Illustration 24) are architecturally similar. Except for their size and the present entrance porches which in the case of the Irish house is an addition and which may well be in the Kelly house, the exteriors are all but identical. Originally, the Irish house had a classic entrance porch with square piers and pilasters and a simple but complete entablature, as shown in Illustration 24. When Captain F. M. Irish built this house about 1850 and moved his family from the log cabin, he may have transferred the name from the previous home. However, on the 1854 Millar map of Iowa City, the words "Rose Hill" are placed in such a position that they indicate the Irish-Hamilton-Turner house previously discussed; yet for years the brick house owned by the late Miss Jane T. Irish, granddaughter of F. M. Irish, has been called "Rose Hill." Real estate appraisement records give 1878 as the date for the

Illustration 23
The Kelly House
432 Reno Street

Kelly house, but this date may be questioned because of its similarity to the Irish house and also because of the date given in the same records for the all-but-identical house next door at 502 Reno Street is 1870. Both the Irish and the Kelly houses have facades with central entrances which have transoms and vertical lights and with two windows on either side of the doorway, five half-windows on the second floor featuring six lights each, broad plain cornices and architraves with returns, and one-story additions to the rear. The first-floor windows of the Irish house have six lights per sash; those on the Kelly house have nine lights in the upper sash and six in the lower. Lintels on both houses are blocks of dressed stone.

The floor plan of the Irish house has a central hall with two rooms on either side. The rear addition provides a fifth room. Upstairs are four bedrooms. The Kelly plan has one large room on either side of the central hall and two large rooms on the second floor. The kitchen is in the ell to the rear.

Illustration 24
The F. M. Irish House
East End, Davenport Street
Photograph from Aurner, *Leading Events in Johnson County Iowa, History*, Vol. 2, page 418

THE SANDERS-MACHOVEC HOUSE

Located on the second lot north of the Kelly house was the weathered clapboard house of the late Mrs. Emma Machovec (Illustration 25). At one time the house must have been the most pretentious house on the street. The earliest notation found concerning the house was that I. N. Sanders owned the property on which the house was located prior to 1866. The real estate appraisement sheets give 1870 as the date for the house. However, because of the architectural similarity of the house to others considered to have been constructed in the 1850's, the assumption is made that the Machovec house dated from that decade. The house was razed in June 1967.

The house was rectangular in plan with a bay window on the right end to the south. It is not known whether the bay was a part of the original structure or not, but its use suggests familiarity with the later Victorian styles. The horizontal clapboarding of the end of the house continued onto the bay. Below the four windows the boarding was vertical; above them was a broad undecorated cornice; at either side of the four windows was a pilaster-like treatment which extended through the cornice to the overhang of the eaves.

Except for the box-like front entrance which probably was an addition,

Illustration 25
The Sanders-Machovec House
516 Reno Street

the house was similar to the other houses discussed in this section. The front doorway was not visible due to the addition. The windows were set within a simple framing; each sash had six panes. The plain cornice and the architrave were placed directly upon the second-floor windows. Both the cornice and the architrave formed a return at the ends. A single undecorated board, placed vertically at the corners and extending from the foundation to the entablature, suggested the use of pilasters at the corners of buildings, which is seen in some interpretations of the Greek Revival style.

THE ENGLERT-POWNALL HOUSE

Another clapboard house which dates from the 1850's is built on the north edge of the city along the old stagecoach road to the west. Since 1928 it has been the residence of Mr. and Mrs. Fred M. Pownall (Illustration 26). The earliest known owner of the property was Clara Englert. She was the wife of Lewis Englert, who operated the city's first brewery. Their son, John J., continued the family business after his father's death and later dealt in ice and wood. The ice house was located on the banks of the Iowa River, a short distance below the house.

Illustration 26
The Englert-Pownall House
1602 North Dubuque Street

At one time the house apparently was a stop on the stagecoach route, and the coaches drove up under the porch on the ground floor to load. When the present owners excavated the earth which formed the ground floor in order to put in cement flooring, two historic items were found. One was a large sign reading "SALOON"; the other was a great circular stone which concealed a bricked-in tunnel that led to a cave in the bluff behind the house. This has led to speculation that the house was at one time a stop on the "underground railway" for smuggling Negro slaves north. Older residents of the area have told the Pownalls that the famous abolitionist, John Brown, who lived at Springdale some fifteen miles east of Iowa City, visited the saloon at one time. The family which maintained the stagecoach stop lived upstairs and, apparently, provided hotel accommodations as well as food and drink.

The foundation of the house which comprises the ground floor story is rubble-laid limestone. The remainder of the house is clapboard. The entrance is centered in the south facade, and there are one-story bay windows at either side. The corners of the house have the same vertical board treatment as the Machovec house. The entrance porch has square channeled columns with pierced decorative brackets forming the capitals. A transom of three lights is above the door, and there is a vertical row of four lights on either side.

The plan is a central hall one with one large room on either side. On the east or right side is a wing housing the kitchen. Upstairs are three bedrooms.

The cornice is simple and broad and has no returns. There is also a broad cornice which follows the line of the gable roof at either end. The one existing chimney which is to the right of the central hall and in the dining room probably was connected to a stove since the house has no fireplaces.

Two additional houses which show a localized interpretation of the Greek Revival style and which have entrances centered in the side parallel to the ridgepole of the gable roof are the Reno-Trott house, 327-329 Brown Street, and the Rohret-Lekin house, 115 North Gilbert Street.

The following three houses present some of the most authentic characteristics of the Greek Revival style that are to be found in nineteenth century Iowa City houses. Each has the entrance to the right of the facade which is on the side parallel to the ridgepole of the gable roof.

THE POWELL-COLDREN AND THE MCCONNELL-BRISTOL-BUCHMAN HOUSES

Two houses so similar that they have often been incorrectly identified are the Solomon Coldren house (non-existent) which was located on the northeast corner of Linn and College Streets and the
former residence of Mrs. Wm. Frank Bristol (Illustrations 27 and 28).
Part of the confusion is due to the fact that the entrance porch on the
Bristol house originally was on the Coldren house and was purchased
by the late Professor and Mrs. Bristol when the Coldren house was
razed in 1925.[25] It has been sold to Elwood Buchman.

On the south side of the Bristol house is a brick with the number
"1857" cut into it. This is the only clue to the possible time when
the house was built. The owner of the property then was Joseph
McConnell, and from the information available to the Bristols when
they purchased the property, they have considered that McConnell
built the house.

Known by older residents of Iowa City as the Coldren home, the
house at the corner of Linn and College Streets probably was constructed for John Powell, who owned the property prior to 1866.
Coldren did not obtain the deed until 1868, according to Johnson
county records. The architectural character of the house suggests
that it was contemporary with the McConnell-Bristol house and perhaps even a little earlier.

Both houses were of brick; both had two windows to the left of the
front entrance and three on the second floor; both had shutters; both
had open porches to the rear. The porch on the McConnell-Bristol
house was bricked in to form an enclosed sun room in 1925.

The classic entrance porch which has served both houses features four
fluted columns with Corinthian capitals. The two interior columns
are round, but the exterior ones are square. Plain channeled pilasters
with simple Doric capitals support the porch where it joins the house.
A complete entablature incorporating a plain architrave, a frieze with
dentils, and a narrow molded cornice rests on the capitals. Above
this is a balustrade rather than a pediment. The balusters are vase-
like in shape.

The lintels of the Powell-Coldren house were of blocks of cut stone.
The McConnell-Bristol house has applied classic wood pediments
which are triangular in shape above the first floor windows. Those
on the second floor have plain molded cornices. The shutters which
remained on the house at the time of purchase were removed by

25 Interview, Mrs. Wm. Frank Bristol, May 5, 1964.

Illustration 27
The Powell-Coldren House (Non-Extant)
304 East College Street
Photographed circa 1920 Courtesy, Fred W. Kent

Illustration 28
The McConnell-Bristol House
606 South Johnson Street

the Bristols and placed in storage in the basement for historical interest.

The cornices of the Powell-Coldren house featured a row of dentils as the frieze. Four groups of coupled decorative brackets were placed across the facade, with one group on the cornice returns at the gable ends. The brackets nearest the corners had pendant drops in addition to the scrolled forms. The McConnell-Bristol cornice uses single brackets evenly spaced and simple moldings. Brackets are also used under the gables.

The Powell-Coldren house had two chimneys on the left side of the house and one on the right. The McConnell-Bristol house has one chimney on the left side which serves the parlor fireplace; there are two chimneys on the wing to the rear.

The plan of the Bristol house has a side entrance hall with a curving staircase. A parlor is to the left of the hall with a dining room adjoining it. Behind the hall is a study. The kitchen and the enclosed sunporch are in the rear wing. The second floor has five rooms, and there are two finished rooms in the attic. The plan of the Coldren house was probably similar if not identical; they may have come from the house pattern books which were the sources used by carpenter-builders of the day, although there is no direct evidence to support this assumption.

THE SANXAY-GILMORE HOUSE

The home of Mrs. Eugene Gilmore, wife of a former president of The University of Iowa (Illustration 29), was originally the home of the Sanxays, long an influential family in the life of the city. The property was received by Frederick Sanxay from the Territory of Iowa on June 16, 1842. Except for a three-year period from 1877 to 1880, the property was held by a member of the family until 1920. The Gilmores purchased the house in 1946. In the Data Sheets the house is dated as 1860, although comparison to houses which were built in the 1850's suggests that it may be a few years older.

The house has a wing with a narrow porch to the right of the main block; otherwise, the facade is similar to the Powell-Coldren and the McConnell-Bristol houses.

The entrance porch is classically correct from the fluted Doric columns to the complete entablature with triglyphs, guttae, mutules, and dentils. The side porch employs piers which have a single square base above which are slender square posts. These have delicate splayed

Illustration 29
The Sanxay-Gilmore House
109 East Market Street

brackets in place of capitals. The cornice of the side porch has a frieze of dentils and coupled brackets.

The main cornice of the house also uses coupled brackets with pendants; these are applied directly over the plain frieze and architrave. The cornice projects deeply. Formerly, the house had shutters at the windows; these were removed by the Gilmores because many were in poor condition.

The foundation of the house is of unusually large blocks of stone, laid in the rubble manner. Mrs. Gilmore has been told that the stones were "left over from the construction of the capitol building."

The main block of the house has a side hall extending through to a kitchen at the rear which is an addition. To the left of the hall are a front and a rear parlor. In the wing to the right is a bedroom, formerly the music room, and immediately behind it is a second bedroom which was the dining room. The original kitchen was probably in the basement. The two parlors have fireplaces as do the two rooms above them on the second floor. Apparently, the other rooms of the house were heated by stoves.

One extant house illustrates the use of a hipped roof in a vernacular interpretation of the Greek Revival style. Also, the residence of Dr.

Illustration 30
The Parker-Lidberg House
1119 East Church Street

Henry Murray pictured in a lithograph drawing in the *Johnson County, Iowa, Atlas,* of 1870 was of this general style.

THE PARKER-LIDBERG HOUSE

The only extant example of a Greek Revival house with the entrance to one side of the facade and with a hipped roof is the Richard Lidberg residence (Illustration 30). The house is a square, box-type structure, dated 1870. The owner of the property at that time was H. L. Parker. On both sides of the house iron stars indicate the presence of tie rods which were frequently used to reinforce brick houses in the nineteenth century. The roof is low-pitched with a broad projecting overhang. An earlier picture circa 1946 shows large single brackets which extended upward from a point parallel to the upper corner of the window framing across the plain broad cornice and under the overhang. The earlier picture also shows, in addition to the present exterior chimney, two interior chimneys instead of just one as in the present house.

The facade of the house is asymmetrically arranged with the entrance to the right. The doorway uses a transom of three panes with three vertical lights on either side, a plan identical to that seen in several houses previously discussed.

The windows have two sashes, each containing six panes. The brick work of the segmentally-arched framings employs two rows of brick headers placed vertically; above these is a projecting row of headers laid horizontally. Originally, there was only one window on the west side of the house, according to the 1946 photograph, but in its present form there are two windows on this side of the house. There are two windows on the east side placed to the rear of the house with one on each floor.

HOUSES OF THE GOTHIC REVIVAL STYLE

The Gothic Revival style with its vertical movement and decorative accents reached the Midwest about 1850. It had been introduced in the East as early as 1800 by Benjamin Henry Latrobe who, paradoxically, is considered to be the father of the Greek Revival style in this country. The Gothic Revival had become highly fashionable by the 1830's and continued popular until shortly after the Civil War of the 1860's.

In the Middlewest local materials were used in Gothic Revival construction most frequently; thus there are many examples in wood throughout the area. In Iowa Gothic Revival houses were most frequently constructed of brick or wood. However, there apparently are no identifiable regional interpretations of the Gothic Revival as there are of the Greek Revival style. This is probably due to the availability of the popular builders' handbooks and their use by carpenters in the East, the South, and the Midwest. The influence of the writings of Andrew Jackson Downing, designer of rural cottages and landscape architect, is also of importance as were those of Alexander Jackson Davis.

Residential plans of the Gothic Revival were both symmetrical and asymmetrical and were modified by the use of rooms which were octagonal or circular in shape and by the addition of bay and oriel windows, towers, turrets, porches, porte-cocheres, and conservatories. Wall openings were typically long and narrow with pointed headings. Roof lines featured steeply pointed gables, often with finials at the peak and with dormer windows. Lacelike bargeboards or vergeboards, jig saw-cut brackets under the eaves, tracery porches, elaborate crestings, and clustered ornamental chimneys were among the decorative features of the style. The exterior treatment often was of vertical boards with battens.

Of the remaining Gothic Revival houses in Iowa City not one employs vertical boarding, a frequently-used construction form of the style. The only building which indicates that this technique was used in the city is Trinity Episcopal Church at the corner of College and Gilbert Streets, built in 1871 (Illustration 84).

THE YOUNKIN-NEGUS HOUSE

The oldest of the Gothic Revival houses in Iowa City is the residence of Lewis H. Negus (Illustration 31) which was constructed in 1863. Archibald C. Younkin probably built the house since deed transfers indicate that he owned the property prior to 1868, although the individual entry is not dated.

Among the Gothic Revival characteristics present in the house are two lancet-shaped windows, one directly over the entrance and centered in a steeply pointed gable, the use of many gabled forms, two dormers on the entrance side of the house, a two-story bay window area, and French doors which substitute for several windows on the first floor.

Three different treatments of gable roofs are seen in the house. The

Illustration 31
The Younkin-Negus House
701 East College Street
Photographed December 15, 1925 Courtesy, Fred W. Kent

outward flare of the dormer gables is repeated on the main gables at the north and south ends of the house and suggests Oriental influence. The gable over the bay window area is pediment-like in form and has a deep projection over the side windows of the bay. The gable over the entrance has a steeper pitch than the other gables and has short returns at the roof line.

Shutters were used at either side of the lancet windows and of the French windows but were not used on the bay. These have been removed, but some are still in existence and are stored at present. Decorative stone caps repeat the form of the pointed windows, and flat lintels form a heading for the French doors.

The original entrance to the house was from the porch which extended partially across the north end of the house and around to the west side. In the Illustration a box-like storm vestibule is visible; this probably was a temporary addition for protection during the winter season and thus concealed the original doorway in this illustration. The porch has been removed in remodeling, but the main doorway is in its original position on the west side. Its treatment is classical, employing two fluted pilasters on either side with a plain entablature and a triangular pediment above the door. The present owners think that this is the original character of the entrance. All of the cornices on the house are broad and simple in the classic manner, and there are no decorative brackets which are so frequently seen on houses of this style. The combination of classical characteristics with details of the Gothic Revival style was frequently seen as the transition was made from the Greek Revival to the Gothic Revival mode of the Victorian era.

THE JACKSON-SWISHER-KEYSER HOUSE

The residence of the late Mr. and Mrs. Clarence W. Keyser (Illustration 32) was constructed in 1877 by Louis H. Jackson, according to county records. For over forty years it was occupied by Stephen A. Swisher, an insurance man, and his family and today is frequently referred to as "the old Swisher place."

The house utilizes more characteristics of the Gothic Revival than any other house in Iowa City. These include the original cruciform plan, the use of bays on the front and right side of the house, porches set into angles formed by the plan, a steeply-pitched gable roof with bargeboards, and numerous decorative details.

Illustration 32
The Jackson-Swisher-Keyser House
120 East Fairchild Street
Photograph not dated Courtesy, Fred W. Kent

The window treatments vary from floor to floor. Those on the first floor have segmental headings with simple framings while those on the second are cut diagonally at the corners. Accentuating the geometric quality of these windows are an angular pediment over the double windows on the front of the house and shallow dormer-like projections cut into the roof over the windows on the sides of the house. These have jerkin-head roofs under which is a scalloped bargeboard which forms an arch. The only pointed-arch windows are found in the points of the gables and serve the attic. Because of this location these windows do not have the vertical quality usually seen in lancet windows.

The bay window on the front of the house has a slanting roof which overhangs a cornice composed of shield-like forms. On the bay window to the right the side walls extend upward above the flat roof, and several decorative forms, including shield-shaped drops and scallops, form a cornice.

The gable roof has an upward flare which is repeated by the wide bargeboards that are pierced by alternating quatrefoils and circles. At the point of the front gable is a large pendant which is cut to appear much like the acanthus leaf form. An identical pendant is used in the gable area above the main entrance porch at the left of the facade. This gable is much smaller than the main gables, but its bargeboard and decorative members are of the same scale as those on the other gables.

Because of the steep pitch of the roof the chimneys are very tall. Two may be seen in Illustration 32, one at the crossing of the gables and the other to its left. The laying of the brick to form decorative caps is also visible. In recent repairing of the chimneys the caps have been simplified.

Originally, the house had two "front" porches as shown in Illustration 32, one of which has been enclosed in order to enlarge the living room.

THE CAVANAUGH-ZETEK HOUSE

Built in 1870, the brick house owned by Miss Rose M. Zetek (Illustration 33) combines Greek Revival and Gothic Revival characteristics, although the latter style dominates the general character of the house.

The entrance porch which is set into an angle formed by the irregular plan of the house is similar to that on the Sanxay-Gilmore house of

Illustration 33
The Cavanaugh-Zetek House
704 Reno Street

the Greek Revival style. It uses plain square pilasters and columns which give visual and actual support to a complete entablature under the flat roof.

The main part of the plan is one and one-half stories in height with a one-story wing to the left of the facade. The one and one-half story or main part of the house has three pointed-arch windows in the facade, each with a cap of voussoirs of brick. The one-story wing also has a pointed-arch window on the facade while two rectangular windows with flat stone lintels are used on the side of the wing. The gable roof of the main part of the house has a narrow bargeboard with a perforated scalloped edging. The remainder of the eaves on the main part of the house has edging of lobe-like forms. The one-story wing has a flat roof with a slight downward slope for drainage and has a narrow cornice used under the overhang of the eaves.

Since James Cavanaugh owned the two lots on which the house is built prior to 1876, having obtained one of them from F. M. Irish, he probably was the original owner of the house.

THE PRICE-SWISHER HOUSE

The Scott Swisher house (Illustration 34) has the asymmetry of plan, the steeply-pitched gables, and the porches with intricately scrolled

Illustration 34
The Price-Swisher House
917 Bowery Street

capitals of the Gothic Revival style but lacks the ornamental bargeboards which are so frequently associated with domestic architecture
of this period. Apparently, there was none on the house since classic
beaded moldings are found at the edge of the overhang. Also characteristic of the style is the use of a semipolygonal bay window with
the sides set at an angle. Its roof with an outward flare suggests
Oriental influence as in the Younkin-Negus house.

The Swishers think that there may have been a porch at the right
side of the facade which balanced the one on the left side since the
enclosed area is an obvious addition. On the second floor the window
headings have a triangular pedimented form but are less high at the
apex than is frequently seen in the earlier Greek Revival style.

Information from the present owners indicates that the house apparently was built for a family by the name of Price in 1870. The Data
Sheet gives 1873 as the date of construction.

Several other Iowa City houses built in the nineteenth century have
Gothic Revival characteristics. Among them are the house owned by
Rose M. Dolezal at 1109 East Fairchild Street, which retains a delicate lace-like bargeboard in addition to square posts, decorative
brackets, a one-story bay window, and many gable forms of the style,
and the C. Emerson Brandt house, 712 East Market Street, which has
an icicle-like bargeboard under the front and side gables as its outstanding Gothic Revival feature. The elongated drops of the bargeboard design also appear under the horizontal eaves.

HOUSES OF THE ANGLO-ITALIAN STYLE

The Anglo-Italian substyle of the Victorian era developed in mid-
nineteenth century and is considered by some writers to have been a
significant statement of American architectural design. One writer
of the time went so far as to intimate that the Italian style was truly
indigenous to America.[26] Historians today, however, consider the style
to be an American interpretation of European style along with the
Franco-American, the Gothic Revival, and the Neo-Jacobean substyles of the Victorian period.

Characteristics of the Italian style, whether it be called "Tuscan
Villa," "Italianate," "Bracketed Villa," "American Bracketed," or "Italian Style Lodge," included asymmetrical arrangement of plan, use of
square towers which often were a story taller than the house, over-

---

[26] Anonymous author of an editorial in *The Architectural Review and American
Builder's Journal*, November, 1868, quoted in Peat, *op. cit.*, p. 96.

hanging eaves supported by single or coupled brackets, tall windows and doors with round-arched headings that had repeating caps, piazzas and verandas, hooded balconies, low-pitched roofs which often combined styles such as gable and mansard, and cupolas, observatories, widow's walks or belvederes topped by scrolled finials, flagpoles, or weathervanes. Not all identifying characteristics would be employed in a single house, and some of them were applied to the simple rectangular forms of the Greek Revival period as has been illustrated in the foregoing section.

In Iowa City three distinct groups of Anglo-Italian houses exist: those with Italian characteristics applied to a basic rectangular form; those with towers, cupolas, and widow's walks; and those without towers, cupolas, and widow's walks.

Houses With Italian Characteristics Applied
To A Basic Rectangular Form

THE CLARK-LOUIS AND THE HERSHIRE-BORDWELL-ALPHA DELTA PI HOUSES

Two houses with entrances to the right of the facade on the side parallel to the ridgepole are the residence of Miss Nena Louis (Illustration 35) and the Percy Bordwell house (Illustration 36) which is no longer extant. Decorative details of the Italian style found in both houses include the front porches which employed slender square columns with decorative capitals and the coupled brackets with pendant drops under the eaves. However, the basic structures, the use of flat lintels, and the treatment of the entrances are in keeping with the Greek Revival style in Iowa City. Both houses also had tall window openings which extended to the floor.

According to information obtained through real estate appraisement, a part of the Louis home was built in 1840. Also included on the Data Sheet are the following comments: "92 yrs.?", "9 Rooms," and "One of the oldest homes in Iowa City." The *Abstract of Original Deeds* records that the original owner of the property was Abraham J. Willis who received the deed from the Territory of Iowa on August 8, 1842. Norwood C. Louis II, great-grandson of John Norwood Clark who obtained the property in 1866, thinks that the rear part of the structure is the original 1840 house, and an 1867 newspaper account indicates that extensive additions to the house were made by Mr. Clark in that year.

County records indicate that the Bordwell house was built in 1875

Illustration 35
The Clark-Louis House
319 South Linn Street

Illustration 36
The Hershire-Bordwell-Alpha Delta Pi House (Non-Extant)
111 East Bloomington Street
Photographed in 1934 Courtesy, Fred W. Kent

by A. J. Hershire, but Professor Bordwell believes parts of it were older because of the ground floor structure. The Alpha Delta Pi sorority purchased the house in 1960. It was razed in 1964.

THE OAKES-WOOD-MILTNER HOUSE

Popularly known as the "Grant Wood house" because of the famed Iowa artist who once owned it and restored it to its original form, the house is today the residence of Mr. and Mrs. E. C. Miltner (Illustration 37). The house was constructed by Nicholas Oakes who established a brickyard near the site of the house in 1856. In addition Oakes manufactured drain tile and probably was the first maker of that product in Johnson County. According to a plaque on the exterior, the house was built in 1858. The Data Sheets compiled circa 1940 while Wood still occupied the house give 1853 as the year of construction, but this probably was a mistake. The assumption is made that the 1858 date is more accurate since Oakes probably built the house of brick that he made himself and because of the plaque.

Illustration 37
The Oakes-Wood-Miltner House
1142 East Court Street

Although the impression made by the facade of the house is one of symmetry, the entrance is actually several feet to the right of center. Italian characteristics include this indication of asymmetry, the coupled brackets with pendants under the eaves, and the first-floor windows which are tall and narrow with framing which extends to the floor level. Instead of the typical decorative caps of the Italian style, the window headings which are segmentally arched have voussoirs of brick. The top rail of shutters repeats the form of the segmental arch. The entrance has a segmental-arched heading above a doorway which features a fanlight, narrow side lights, and paneling that is classical in character.

The house, made up of twelve rooms, has a more or less typical nineteenth century floor plan which had two parlors, an entrance hall, a dining room, a kitchen, and a pantry on the first floor and five bedrooms on the second floor. In Grant Wood's restoration of the house in 1936 a porch which had been added to the original house was removed.

Cast-iron star supports indicating tie-rods are visible on the facade of the house at the second-floor level.

The white picket fence was a part of the original architecture of the house and employs finials on top of the large square posts that are similar in design to the pendants on the eave brackets.

THE WILLIAMS-SCHOMP-WARNER HOUSE

The clapboard house owned by Arthur Schomp and Eleanor Warner (Illustration 38) probably was a farmhouse at the time it was constructed since it is several blocks east of the boundaries of the original town. County records show that the house was built in 1858, apparently by John Williams who is listed as owner of the property before 1866.

The facade is formally oriented, and the central doorway has a transom of four lights across the top of the opening and three vertical lights on either side. The windows on either side of the entrance have framing beneath the openings as well as shutters extending to the floor level, indicating knowledge of the window form often used in the Italian style. Above the second-floor windows are headings which are a flattened triangular pediment form.

The veranda which extends across the facade is the most ornamented part of the house. It is composed of four slender square columns supporting a narrow cornice which has a delicate scalloped edging of stalactite-like drops below a frieze of dentils. Small pendants appear

Illustration 38
The Williams-Schomp-Warner House
1232 East College Street

at the corners of the frieze and at regular intervals around the porch roof.

Other details of the house are chaste and restrained with little or no decoration.

THE COCHRAN-DENNIS HOUSE AND THE HUTCHINSON-SHAW HOUSE

Two houses, similar to the Williams-Schomp-Warner house in basic form and in the use of one-story verandas extending across the facade, are the Cochran-Dennis house (Illustration 39) and the Hutchinson-Shaw house (now called the Jefferson Street Apartment House, Illustration 40.) According to real estate appraisement records, the former was constructed in 1865 by M. B. Cochran and the latter in 1883 by Robert Hutchinson.

Both houses are formally oriented with the entrance centered in the facade. The verandas of both houses have square coupled columns, each with decorative capitals. Those on the Dennis house have an outward flare and are delicately and intricately scrolled; those on the apartment house are simple and square in character beneath a cornice which combines scrolled brackets and dentils.

The roof of the Dennis house is unusually low-pitched for a gable roof in the northern part of the country. Under its overhang are elaborate

Illustration 39
The Cochran-Dennis House
412 North Clinton Street

Illustration 40
The Hutchinson-Shaw House
318 East Jefferson Street

coupled brackets which have no cornice behind them but rest directly upon the brick. The apartment building has a typical Midwestern gable roof with a broad cornice board and cornice returns at the gable ends.

The first-floor windows of both houses extend to the floor, and those on the Dennis house are rectangular in form while the apartment house windows are segmentally arched. The central window on the second floor of the Dennis house repeats the form of those on the first floor in height; the other two are less deep. Flat stone lintels are used above all windows in the facade. On the apartment house the second-floor windows, including those in the bay, have segmental arches with decorative caps.

As was so frequently done in the nineteenth century, major attention was lavished upon the facade of the house with the other exposures allowed to develop with little thought to the finished appearance of those areas.

THE KAUFFMAN-WALKER HOUSE

Although the present impression made by the brick house at 304 South Summit Street is that of a combination of Greek Revival and Anglo-Italian characteristics, the house as it originally was planned was of the latter style, according to a 1927 picture (Illustration 41).

Illustration 41
The Kauffman-Walker House
304 South Summit Street
Photographed in 1927 Courtesy, Fred W. Kent

The removal of the veranda with its very elaborate post brackets and its bracketed cornice and the addition of a classic pilastered and pedimented treatment around the entrance cause this confusion. Italianate characteristics still remaining include the main cornice which combines a band of dentils and coupled brackets with pendants. The arrangement of the brackets alternates pairs which extend below the cornice and rest on the brick wall surface with pairs which are attached only to the cornice. The structure has a one-story bay window with a bracketed cornice on the right side of the house, and in the gable over the entrance is a pointed arch window with a dressed stone cap and a keystone. Other windows have flat stone lintels.

The house was constructed in 1883 by Levi Kauffman who developed the surrounding addition to the city which is named for him. Today it has been remodeled into apartments by the present owner, Mrs. Myron Walker.

THE RITTENMEYER-CHELF HOUSE

Another house similar to those included in this section is the Paul C. Chelf residence (Illustration 42). Built of brick in 1879 by Francis X.

Illustration 42
The Rittenmeyer-Chelf House
630 East Fairchild Street

Rittenmeyer, the house has as its distinctive feature the veranda which has a balustrade and a soffit grille with an open repeat design. Its general character is reminiscent of Chinese lattice work with its geometric quality.

Houses With Towers and Cupolas

THE WILLS-CLARK-CURRIER HALL ANNEX HOUSE
AND THE HIGHT-HICKEY HOUSE

Only two examples of the Anglo-Italian style with square towers have been located, and one has been razed and the other remodeled so that most of the Italian characteristics, including the tower, have been removed.

The house at 325 North Clinton Street (Illustration 43) apparently was built in 1871 by D. F. Wills who sold it to Ezekial Clark in 1873. Clark held it until 1910. In 1941 it was purchased by The University of Iowa and used as an annex to Currier Hall, women's dormitory in the adjacent block, until it was razed in late 1955 or early 1956 to provide space for a new women's housing unit, Burge Hall.

The house was truly a mansion of its time. Constructed of brick, the

Illustration 43
The Wills-Clark-Currier Hall Annex House (Non-Extant)
325 North Clinton Street
Photographed circa 1947 Courtesy, Fred W. Kent

two-and-a-half story house featured a central tower which extended half-a-story above the roofline and was topped by a mansard roof on its slanting apex. Round windows with boldly projecting framing were placed in the sides of the mansard area. On the facade of the tower in the third-story area was a round-arched window that broke the cornice line of the tower. The tower was divided by a string-course and an ornamental brick treatment at the point of demarcation between the second and third stories. Two slender round-arched windows which had caps with incised decoration were the tower openings on the second floor. Other windows on the second floor were larger in scale and had similar caps except for the addition of a nonfunctioning keystone.

The gable roof of the main parts of the house had a wide overhang and a very broad cornice with coupled brackets. The gable over the projecting bay at the left of the tower had deep returns and rested directly upon triple windows in the half-story area. The two outside windows were cut diagonally to conform to the cornice and at the same time provide maximum light to the interior. A shed dormer was placed on the gable roof to the right of the tower.

The broad veranda across the facade on the first floor may have been a part of the original structure, but its general character and lack of typical Italian decoration suggest that it was an addition or that it had been remodeled.

The second house that is known to have had a tower is now the residence of Mrs. Bessie C. Hickey (Illustration 44). The house was built circa 1860 by Eliza J. Hight.

Pictured before it was remodeled, the house had a typical Tuscan Villa square tower set in an angle of the building. Also typical of the style was the shallow hipped roof with broad overhang as the conclusion of the tower. Other Italianate features included were the fringed hood placed over the window in the second floor of the tower, the bay windows to the left of the facade and on the right side of the house, and the bracketed treatment of the cornices.

An unusual feature of the Hickey house was the treatment above the second story window in the gable area to the left of the tower. A round-arched window was set into a projecting area which rested upon the roof of the bay window below. This area was topped by a deeply projecting gable which repeated the line of the main roof of the house a short distance above it. Also unusual was the frame-like decoration placed on the tower above the fringed hood. On the second floor of the right side of the house was an elongated Palladian win-

Illustration 44
The Hight-Hickey House
228 East Church Street
Photographed circa 1947 Courtesy, Fred W. Kent

dow, a characteristic most frequently associated with the Georgian style of the eighteenth century.

In the remodeling of the house all of the Italianate and other decorative members were eliminated, and the rear part of the structure behind the bay window area was removed. The tower was cut down to the level of the eaves and finished with a flat roof surrounded by a balustrade.

THE C. D. CLOSE HOUSE

The C. D. Close residence (Illustration 45), built in 1874 at a cost of over $15,000 according to a newspaper item in that year, was one of the mansions of Iowa City. August Hazelhorst is known to have been the contractor for the house. Close followed a common practice of the time and built his home near the family businesses, a linseed oil company and a glove factory. The linseed oil company was located diagonally across the street and the glove enterprise a few blocks away. The house has been extensively remodeled and today serves as headquarters for the Johnson County Department of Social Welfare. At one time it housed the Acacia fraternity.

Many of the characteristics of the Italian style were removed in the remodeling, including the widow's walk and a glassed-in cupola, the balcony with its fringe-like hood to the left of the entrance, the decorative front porch, and the balustrade over the bay window at the right of the entrance. A pair of rectangular double-sash windows were substituted for the oval-shaped oculus window in the front gable, but an original one remains in the side gable.

The extremely broad cornice decorated with large alternating single and coupled brackets, modillions between the brackets, and horizontal panels incorporating applied diamond shapes encircles the entire house at the roof line and is repeated on the one-story front bay window as well as on a two-story bay on the right side of the house. The window headings vary; some are round-arched and others are segmental-arched, but all have decorative caps which extend approximately a third of the length of the window.

The house is raised on a high ashlar stone foundation which has a water table of dressed rock. The brick was originally red in color but is now painted gray. The chimney adjacent to the cupola was very tall in order to prevent smoke from interfering with the view and for safety.

The interior of the house featured an open stair well which extended from the first floor to the observatory, marble fireplaces, and massive glass chandeliers. The flooring was of hardwood on the first floor and of softwood on the second.

THE LYON HOUSE

No longer standing is the E. C. Lyon house (Illustration 46) which in the 1920's served as the home of the Delta Chi fraternity of The University of Iowa. No date has been found for the construction of the house, but the 1854 Millar map of Iowa City includes an outline of a square structure with a rear addition on the Van Buren Street site and labels it "Roanoke, E. C. Lyon." This suggests that the house had been built prior to the date of the map. Aurner recorded that Lyon and his brother owned the Iowa City Manufacturing Company circa 1846 and constructed a dam across the Iowa River in the present Coralville vicinity which provided power for their mill.

The house was formally oriented and two-and-one-half stories high with a cupola on top of a roof that appears to be flat or nearly so. As a result of the angle from which the picture was taken, there is difficulty in determining whether the roof was flat or was a shallow hipped one. The cupola was six-sided and had round-arched windows, a flagpole on top, and a bracketed cornice under the overhang of the

Illustration 45
The Close House
538 South Gilbert Street
Photographed circa 1920 Courtesy, Fred W. Kent

Illustration 46
The Lyon House (Non-Extant)
617 South Van Buren Street
Photographed circa 1914 Courtesy, Fred W. Kent

flat roof. The main cornice extended across most of the half-story area and was pierced at regular intervals by eyebrow windows. Coupled brackets with stalactite-like pendants extended vertically across the cornice and concluded with a small extension onto the brick wall beneath it. Small brackets or perhaps modillions were spaced between the brackets, and under these were horizontal panels with rounded corners. This cornice treatment was also used on the wing on the left side of the house. The windows were round- or segmental-arched and were capped with headings that were in bold relief against the wall and had a central motif suggesting the acanthus leaf form.

The entrance porch had square channeled columns and pilasters under its flat roof. The treatment of the porch cornice was similar to that of the main one. A long veranda paralleled the rear wing of the house.

The foundation and its projecting water table were composed entirely of dressed stone.

THE GOTCH-PRICE-SWENSON HOUSE

Similar in basic form of structure to the Lyon house is the home of the Carl Swenson family (Illustration 47). The Data Sheets state that the house was "60+" years of age at the time of their compilation

Illustration 47
The Gotch-Price-Swenson House
1110 East Kirkwood Avenue
Photographed circa 1914 Courtesy, Fred W. Kent

which would date the house circa 1880. Originally, the house had eleven rooms.

The main part of the house is square in form, and there is a long rear wing with a veranda along one side. This is now an enclosed porch. The hipped roof was topped by a widow's walk which had openings in the shape of quatrefoils in the balustrade and heavy corner posts which were bracketed and had pointed finials. This feature has been entirely removed.

The intricate cornice treatment combines a regular spacing of large coupled brackets with smaller brackets between, each of which has two stalactite-like drops. There is no cornice board; thus, the larger brackets rest directly upon the brick wall.

The fenestration of the house employs round-arched windows on the second floor and segmental-arched windows on the first floor with the exception of the semipolygonal bay which has narrow round-arched windows with dressed stone caps that are flush with the wall. The headings of all other windows are simple in detail but boldly projecting. On the second floor directly over the entrance is a triple window which has round arches as headings for each of its sections. The veranda on the front of the house has both single and coupled square columns with bases which have an outward flare that is produced by the application of four thin curvilinear brackets. The cornice board springs from the capitals in segmental arches, and the eave treatment repeats the smaller brackets of the main cornice. The recessed entrance has a large round-arched shape with lights repeating this form.

This house is one of two in Iowa City which has corner quoins of dressed stone as one of its decorative details. The foundation is of limestone laid in the ashlar manner and has a projecting water table of dressed stone.

Apparently, the house was built by a Mr. Gotch who was co-owner of a large meat packing and processing plant. Later the M. F. Price family owned the house, and its members are those most frequently associated with the property by older Iowa City residents.

Houses Without Towers, Cupolas, and Widow's Walks

Included in this section are houses without some of the most outstanding of the Anglo-Italian characteristics but which are, nevertheless, typical of a great many Midwestern houses of the style. They retain such decorative details as elaborate brackets under wide eaves, verandas, and arched windows with decorative headings and may be either symmetrical or nonsymmetrical in plan.

THE REECE-FLORA HOUSE

Illustrating the use of the projecting central pavilion of the Italian style is the frame residence of the Robert Flora family (Illustration 48). The pavilion terminates in an open pediment with returns which are supported by scrolled brackets. Between the returns is a square window with a shallow arched heading, and on either side is a pair of eyebrow windows. Other windows in the house are rectangular in shape and have dog-eared frames. Comparison to an early photograph in the Kent files shows that the form on the roof which repeats the pavilion pediment is an addition to the original house. Over the eyebrow windows is a fringed edging, and on either side of these windows on the cornice board are plain beveled panels.

The veranda extends across the facade and has square posts with intricately scrolled brackets which form the capitals. On either side of the main block of the house are small one-story projections, a semipolygonal bay on the left, and a rectangular wing on the right.

The house was constructed in 1883 for Catherine Reece who is listed in county records as the owner of the property from 1881 to 1896 when it was sold to O. H. Byington.

THE CLAPP-KELLER HOUSE

Also constructed in 1883 was the building presently housing the Keller apartments and formerly the Delta Upsilon fraternity (Illustration 49). Apparently, the house was built for P. Agnes Clapp and her husband, although the date for their original ownership of the property is not clear in county records. They are listed as selling the property in 1889. Originally composed of thirteen rooms, the house has undergone extensive remodeling including removal of the brackets with drops under the eaves, and the veranda and porte-cochere which were examples of Italianate influence, particularly in their brackets and balustrade turnings and in the round arch forms employed on the roof of the porte-cochere. Characteristics of the style which remain today are the coupled arched windows over the single arched doorway, eyebrow windows which perforate the cornice board on either side of the house, and a semipolygonal bay on the right side of the house.

Illustration 48
The Reece-Flora House
415 South Summit Street

Illustration 49
The Clapp-Keller House
725 East College Street
Photographed circa 1920 Courtesy, Fred W. Kent

THE DEY HOUSE

A third frame house showing characteristics of the Anglo-Italian style was built in 1857 by Peter A. Dey, a railroad commisisoner for the State of Iowa and two-time president of the First National Bank of Iowa City. The house at present is occupied by The University of Iowa's Institute of Public Affairs (Illustration 50). The Dey family moved into the twelve-room house in September of 1857, and it was the family home until purchased by The University of Iowa. Part of Outlot 31 on which the house stands was bought in 1923 with the remainder obtained in 1937.

Its most distinctive Italianate features are the veranda with columns formed of triple shafts springing from a single base, the round-arched window in the gable, the scrolled brackets under the eaves, and the delicate iron cresting on the central part of the roof. Visible in Illustration 50 are false shuttered "windows," one on each floor of the left side of the house. Neither opens into the interior. Such treatment was sometimes introduced in the nineteenth century to produce a more pleasing effect on the exterior.

THE LOVELACE-SCHEUERMAN-BROWN HOUSE

The residence of Merle E. Brown (Illustration 51) was constructed by a Mr. Lovelace [Loveless?], perhaps a descendant of the gentleman who constructed the Henry C. Nicking house. Real estate records date the house as 1882, but former residents, the Milton (Sharm) Scheuermans, believe that it probably was built in the early 1870's because of information given to them by a grandson of Lovelace. He also gave them the picture used in Illustration 51.

Many of the Anglo-Italian characteristics of the house have been removed, including the veranda which had coupled posts with intricately-cut brackets and the large paired brackets with pendants under the eaves. Also, the trefoil window in the front gable has been replaced by a three-section horizontal window. The front entrance which projected onto the porch remains and shows its early form including oblique corners in which are semi-arched vertical windows. The second-floor windows have projecting segmental-arched pediments, and there are deep cornice returns which originally appear to have extended to a point over the center of the pediments of the windows nearest the corners of the area. A two-story bay window area is placed on either side of the house, and these formerly had a cornice treatment which included the very large brackets with pendants.

Illustration 50
The Dey House
507 North Clinton Street

Illustration 51
The Lovelace-Sherman-Brown House
820 Kirkwood Avenue
Photograph not dated
Courtesy, Mr. and Mrs. Milton (Sharm) Scheuerman

THE KOZA-SAINT WENCESLAUS RECTORY AND THE
GEIGER-WESLEY FOUNDATION HOUSE

Two brick houses of the Anglo-Italian style which have gable ends facing the street are the rectory of the Saint Wenceslaus Catholic Church (Illustration 52) and the headquarters for the Wesley Foundation of the First Methodist Church (Illustration 53). A newspaper article indicates that the rectory was built as a private dwelling in 1882 by Joseph Koza. It was purchased by the parish in 1893. The Wesley Foundation building was erected in 1870 by Anton Geiger, according to county records.

The rectory is the more elaborate of the two buildings and includes more characteristics that are Italian in character. Its projecting window caps with incised designs contrast to the plain segmental-arched headings at Wesley House.

The rectory entrance features a hooded overdoor supported on either side by a very large decorative bracket and has a low lacy iron railing cresting the roof. The heading over the transom is similar to those above the windows. The door itself is not centered in the opening but is placed to the left with a single vertical light above a plain wood panel filling the space at the right. The entrance at Wesley House is recessed but otherwise is treated identically to the windows.

Each house has a small window in the gable area. That on the rectory is a combination of a trefoil and a triangle, and that on Wesley House is round with a plain heading encircling it.

The cornice of Wesley House is somewhat more elaborate than that on the rectory. The former uses scrolled coupled brackets with dentils as its frieze while the latter has coupled triangular-shaped brackets which have no openings placed against a frieze of vertical paneling. The rectory has cornice returns whereas Wesley House does not. Both houses have additions to the main block of the house. Those on the rectory are two-story rectangular bays on either side while Wesley House has a one-story semipolygonal bay on the left side and a two-story rectangular bay on the right. Both houses also have shallow ashlar foundations with a broad projecting water table of dressed stone.

THE COCHRAN HOUSE

The brick house built by James C. Cochran (Illustration 54) is no longer standing, but it apparently was one of the more unusual of the Iowa City houses with Italianate characteristics. The roofs of the veranda and the one-story bay were curved forms, and the shape of

Illustration 52
The Koza-Saint Wenceslaus House
618 East Davenport Street
Photographed circa 1947 Courtesy, Fred W. Kent

Illustration 53
The Geiger-Wesley Foundation House
213 East Market Street

Illustration 54
The Cochran House (Non-Extant)
314 South Clinton Street
Photographed in June 1947 Courtesy, Fred W. Kent

the cornice under the porch eaves suggests forms used in openings of buildings of Middle Eastern countries. Other decorative components of this cornice were a band of dentils and single brackets which rested on the capitals of the supporting columns. The columns themselves were reeded and had the shape of a quatrefoil, resting on octagonal bases.

All of the first- and second-floor windows including those in the bay had segmental headings. The bay windows were set into a wood framing, but the others had curved dressed stone headings which were carved to suggest that they were composed of six stones. The first-floor windows to the left of the entrance had sills near the floor and were shuttered. A window in the shape of the quatrefoil was placed in the gable facing the street with a simple round oculus window used in the side gable. The front gable window had a heading treated like the windows below it, while a simple heading of brick encircled the round window.

The cornice under the broad eaves had returns at the gable ends and included a frieze of dentils between heavy scrolled brackets with square tapering pendants. The picture shows that the brackets under the side gable were not identical to the others but had acanthus

Illustration 55
The Cannon-Gay House
320 Melrose Avenue

leaves applied to the vertical member and pendants which also had a leaf form.

Cochran, a native of Glasgow, Scotland, began construction of the family residence in 1869. Black walnut was used to finish the interior of the house, including the doors and casings.

THE CANNON-GAY HOUSE

The brick residence of Charles W. Gay (Illustration 55) is an example of a house with Italian influence which is L-shaped in plan with the projection toward the street. Built in 1884 by a Mr. Cannon, the house has the projecting wing at the left of the facade and also has a second projection which is more shallow in the center of the facade to accommodate the entrance. This area has a flat roof at the eave line of the adjoining gables which suggests that a tower may have existed there at one time, but no evidence has been found indicating this.

All of the windows on the front of the house are paired round-arched windows, and each has a heading of brick voussoirs set flush with the wall surface and a keystone of dressed stone which projects slightly. A round oculus window with brick voussoirs and four keystones framing it is set into the front gable. The main cornice has a wide overhang under which are coupled brackets. An unusual feature is the cutting of the cornice board to fit around the headings of the windows. The square porch posts have elaborate jig saw-cut brackets.

THE WILLIAMS-UNASH HOUSE

The house at 602 West Benton Street owned by Florence Unash (Illustration 56) is a square house of the style with a veranda on two sides, a cornice using single evenly-spaced brackets, and shed dormers with round-arched windows. It was built in 1890 and was at one time the residence of J. H. Williams, proprietor of the Iowa City Commercial College. A picture in the 1898 Iowa City commercial magazine shows that the house had a cupola at that time.

THE CLARK-BUNGE HOUSE

Built circa 1874 by Florence A. Clark, the house now owned by Dr. Raymond G. Bunge (Illustration 57) has a rectangular bay on the front of the house and flat stone lintels over the windows. The flat roof of the bay is on a level with the cornice returns of the main gable and has a broad overhang under which is a single bracket in the center of the area and coupled brackets at the corners. The main cornice has a similar bracket treatment. There is no opening on the front gable, but a round oculus window is placed in the gables on the right and left sides of the house. The veranda has simple, square columns and capitals, an undecorated cornice, and no balustrade.

Several other houses of the Italian style are worthy of mention. They include the Glyde B. Miller house, 906 East Market Street, and the Deming Apartment House, 504 East Bloomington Street, both of which are architecturally similar to the Clark-Bunge house. In addition, the former residence of Governor Samuel J. Kirkwood, 1101 Kirkwood Avenue, is now the home of Professor and Mrs. E. W. Chittenden. Built in 1864, it is austerely plain in comparison with other houses of the style; yet the basic plan and the wide overhang of the eaves with typical coupled brackets are Italian in origin.

HOUSES OF THE FRANCO-AMERICAN STYLE

The Franco-American style was fashionable in the United States between 1860 and 1880, with its peak of acceptance being about 1870. Based on the style of the French Second Empire, the principal distinguishing feature was the mansard roof cut by dormers which might be rectangular, pointed and gabled, or rounded. Frequently, corbels

Illustration 56
The Williams-Unash House
602 West Benton Street

Illustration 57
The Clark-Bunge House
829 Kirkwood Avenue

were placed at either side of the dormer, appearing to support it. Many materials were used, but brick was the national favorite for the style. The slope of the mansard roof could be straight, concave, convex, or even an S-curve. The overall style employed many decorative features, including iron crestings on the roof, decorative moldings, corner quoins, brackets under the eaves, cupolas, and window panes of colored glass. There was frequent use of tall French windows and doors. The plan of these houses was often an asymmetrical one; there were at least two floors and sometimes three; and many such residences had deep porches across the front, sometimes extending around to one side.

In Iowa City today only six examples of the Franco-American style remain, and two houses of the style have been demolished since early 1962. Of these eight, three would be considered the "mansion" type of dwelling, indicating a fashionable acceptance of the French style in Iowa City.

THE CARSON-ALPHA PHI SORORITY HOUSE AND THE BOAL-MAINE HOUSE

Two mansions on East College Street, the Carson-Alpha Phi house (Illustration 58) and the Boal-Maine house (Illustration 59) are similar but not identical examples of the Franco-American style. The Carson house was completed in 1875 for Thomas C. Carson, a dealer in agricultural implements and a banker. The Boal-Maine house has not been accurately dated, but an item in the Iowa City *Daily Evening Press* of May 1, 1871, indicates that the house was built prior to that year since the owner, Mr. George Boal, was described as adding a third story and a mansard roof at the time. Also the mansard was called "the first in this city." Boal dealt in real estate and also was connected with the early railroad systems serving Iowa City.

Both houses are three stories high, both have a symmetrical facade, and both have some irregular projections of mass such as one- or two-story additions to the rear and bay windows. Both mansard roofs have a concave slope, and the dormers are rounded with rounded decorative caps. The Carson house has corbeled supports at either side of the dormers; the Boal-Maine house has classic columns with Corinthian capitals supporting the arched dormer pediments. The mansard area of both houses is covered with shingles laid in alternating bands of rectangular and diamond-shaped patterns. Both have porches across the front, the roofs of which are supported by slender square columns which have decorative splayed brackets at their conclusion.

Illustration 58
The Carson-Alpha Phi House
906 East College Street
Photographed March, 1927 Courtesy, Fred W. Kent

Illustration 59
The Boal-Maine House
806 East College Street

The Carson house employs a projecting central pavilion in the facade which culminates in a tower that extends several feet above the roofline. The mansard roof of the tower contrasts with the surrounding roof area in that it is convex in form. The tower originally was topped by a delicate iron cresting. On the second floor is a doorway in the pavilion area which is covered by a projecting arched hood. An earlier Kent picture shows that a low railing was placed on the porch roof, giving the appearance of a balcony to this doorway area.

All of the windows of the Boal-Maine house have segmental headings and simple framings. Those of the Carson house vary from floor to floor. All of the third floor windows have semi-circular arched headings. Those on the front of the second floor are also half-arched, but the ones on the sides of the house use segmental arches as headings. The window caps are rounded and decorative. The windows of the first floor are rectangular in shape with rounded corners at the top and flat decorative lintels. One exception was a window on the west side of the house which had a door-like opening below it that extended to the floor. This was planned in order to give access to a conservatory which was never constructed, according to Mrs. George S. Carson, Sr., daughter-in-law of the first owner. This feature is not visible today due to recent additions.

The decorative cornice at the top of the mansard roof of the Carson house uses bands of shallow dentils and of scallops combined with simple moldings. The same cornice area of the central tower has three decorative elements, a band of scallops at the bottom surmounted by a row of small dentils which is topped by an elongated interpretation of the classic bead and reel design. The wide cornice below the overhang of the roof features closely spaced decorative brackets above a row of scallops. Similar but smaller bracket forms are used on the cornice of the porch.

The treatment of the cornices of the Boal-Maine house is not as elaborate as that of the Carson house. Small dentils are placed under a comparatively wide overhang at the top of the roof. The cornice separating the second and third floors also features small dentils and in addition has four regularly spaced groups of coupled brackets across the front. The porch cornice is shallow and void of decoration other than decorative pendant forms which appear between the splayed capitals of the square columns.

The Boal-Maine house, presently owned by the heirs of A. E. Maine who acquired the property in 1891, has been remodeled to accommodate apartments. At one time the Carson house was also remodeled into apartments, but in the current remodeling the Alpha Phi sorority has restored several rooms on the main floor to their original plan. This includes the small reception room at the right of the hall with its original black marble fireplace and the living room which is behind it.

THE COX HOUSE

A third brick example of the Franco-American style was the historic Cox mansion (Illustration 60) which was demolished in November of 1964. According to Mrs. George Harold Rigler, the former Sarah Cox, the house was built in 1856 by a Colonel Culbertson and purchased by her grandfather, Thomas Jefferson Cox, in 1865. Colonel Culbertson has not been identified, and his name does not appear in the *Johnson County Transfer Records* as the original owner of the property nor as a subsequent owner. T. J. Cox was a federal land agent and came to Iowa City in the company of Samuel J. Kirkwood. The two were associated in the real estate business. The house was in the Cox family for three generations, being deeded from T. J. Cox to his son, Arthur J. Cox, in 1944, and finally to the heirs on the death of Mrs. Arthur J. Cox in January of 1964.

Illustration 60
The Cox House (Non-Extant)
104 East Market Street
Photographed April 1955 Courtesy, Fred W. Kent

An unusual feature of the house was the depth of the mansard roof; it was considerably more shallow than the familiar prototype and thus did not provide for a full third story. Also unusual were the three triangular dormer windows in the mansard roof on the south facade of the house. A single triangular dormer was also used on the west side of the roof. The roof, made of slate, was crested with a delicate lace-like iron grillwork around its periphery.

The roof had a wide overhang which was composed of bands of rounded moldings separated by a row of shallow, closely spaced dentils. The broad frieze beneath this cornice combined two rows of incised Latin cross forms that were flower-like in interpretation with alternating coupled and single brackets which were angular in form. The front of the house featured a broad veranda which extended across the front and around to the east side. Square columns with four applied brackets forming each capital supported the porch roof. The frieze of the cornice was composed of a band of scallops. The doorway was framed with rounded moldings and had an elongated bracket at either side supporting the flat cornice. The doorknob of the house had the word, "Iowa" engraved on it.

The majority of the windows of the house were of the single pane, two-sash type, had flat lintels and sills of dressed stone, and used louvered shutters. One exception was a large arched window on the first floor on the left side of the house which served the music room. The stained glass in the half-circular arch was in a sunburst pattern and combined clear and colored glass. The lintel of this window was formed of bricks laid in a radiating pattern with a nonfunctional projecting stone keystone at the top.

The floor plan was an asymmetrical one featuring a paneled hallway with a graceful oak stairway. The interior moldings of the house were classic in character, employing broad projecting cornices and bands of egg-and-dart motif and of dentils. These were added to the house when it was remodeled in 1920.[27]

The house was constructed of red sand brick which came from a quarry near the present cemetery in the northeast part of town, according to Thomas G. Cox, grandson of Thomas J. Cox. During the demolition the discovery of the use of square handcrafted nails in the construction of the house was made.

---

[27] Interview, Mrs. George Harold Rigler, February 11, 1967.

THE JOHNSON-BODINE-LANG HOUSE

Located on the north edge of Iowa City on Prairie du Chien Road is
the house built by Iowa City's first brickmaker, Sylvanus Johnson,
and presently owned by the Allen N. Langs (Illustration 61). "Pine-
hurst" was built in 1857, a year after the Cox house. Apparently,
Johnson was a civic-minded individual for the Aurner history indicates that he served on the school board, was a trustee of the early
Mechanic's Institute and of the Davenport and Iowa City Railway,
and donated liberally to the proposed Iowa City Female Collegiate
Institute and to the erection of every church built in Iowa City.

A native of Connecticut, Johnson is said to have planned his house
as much like his former home in that state as possible. Even the great
pine trees on the property were brought from Connecticut as mere
slips by Johnson. Old-timers of Iowa City told a former owner, the
late Professor Joseph H. Bodine, that the house originally featured a
"widow's walk," another indication of Johnson's desire to emulate
houses in his native state.

Built of brick which came from Johnson's kiln on the site, the house
is two stories high and is square in shape with an added kitchen ell.

Illustration 61
The Johnson-Bodine-Lang House
Prairie du Chien Road
Photographed September 25, 1952 Courtesy, Fred W. Kent

The east facade is formally arranged with two windows flanking the central doorway on either side on the first floor. Across the entire front of the house and extending around onto the south or left side is a veranda which suggests the French *galerie* form. Seven slender square pillars support the porch roof, and each has two splayed brackets and a small pendant drop which combine to form its capital. The slanting mansard roof is composed of bands of alternating rectangular and fish-scale shingles. The three dormer windows on the facade have simple triangular pediments which project strongly from the roof, and each has a curved swelling at the top and bottom of the framing that suggests the French use of corbels. The top of the roof is not flat as in the other Iowa City houses of the Franco-American style previously discussed but rises in the center, giving the effect of a low flattened gable. A half-window of three vertical lights is placed in the point of the gable above the central dormer.

The cornice between the first and second floors has a wide overhang under which are simple, closely-spaced brackets. The moldings are rounded. The cornice at the top of the mansard also projects and uses simple moldings.

The entrance to the house from the veranda is set within a rectangular frame with three vertical lights on either side and three horizontal lights above the door. The framing is restrained and classical in inspiration.

The first-floor windows are simply framed and have sills of dressed stone but have no lintels. The sash windows have one large pane per sash. The windows are paired in the dormers and are divided by a vertical mullion. Each sash has four panes.

THE LEWIS-KOSER HOUSE AND THE FRACKER-RATE HOUSE

Two two-story frame houses on Clinton Street were built in the 1880's in the French style, the Lewis-Koser house (Illustration 62) which was razed in 1962 to provide the site for the Kate Daum House addition to Burge Hall, women's dormitory at The University of Iowa, and the Fracker-Rate house (Illustration 63) which is still standing. The former had an unusual feature not seen in other houses of the French style in Iowa City, the small flattened gables which were placed above the cornice of the mansard roof on all four sides of the main block of the house. It also had small corbel-like supports at either side of its dormer windows.

The Fracker-Rate house has two front entrances located on the porches on either side of the central projecting wing of the house.

Illustration 62
The Lewis-Koser House (Non-Extant)
227 North Clinton Street
Photographed in 1962

Illustration 63
The Fracker-Rate House
625 South Clinton Street

The roof is flat, and all windows have segmental-arched headings. The other two Iowa City houses which retain the mansard roof form are the residence of Miss Regina M. Schneider, 502 Iowa Avenue, and the preschool of the Institute of Child Behavior and Development, The University of Iowa, at 10 East Market Street. Both structures have undergone remodeling.

HOUSES OF THE NEO-JACOBEAN STYLE

Many names, "Queen Anne Revival," "Free Classic," "Modern American Renaissance," "Free Jacobean," and others have been used to designate the style which developed in this country late in the 1870's and which had been initiated early in that decade in England by Richard Norman Shaw. Although the style was at first based upon the English architecture of Queen Anne's time in the early eighteenth century, many of its characteristics came from earlier periods including medieval, late Tudor, and Jacobean elements. This has prompted Peat to promote the use of the term "Neo-Jacobean," thus implying not only the inclusion of earlier features but also a revitalized and an American interpretation of the style.[28]

Informality of both the plan and the arrangement of elevations and openings set the keynote for the style. Frequent use of projecting wings and bays, a characteristic which may be traced to the late medieval English styles, gave the exteriors a freedom of appearance which contrasted with the familiar square and rectangular plans of preceding styles. The projecting sections, frequently chamfered, produced irregular roof contours combining hipped and gabled forms, and to these were often added dormers, gables, and chimneys which were found in Tudor or Jacobean architecture. Window treatments were varied, and wall surfaces included clapboard or siding, a psuedo half-timber technique (sometimes termed paneling or banding), brick, and shingles cut in various patterns. Often two or more of these methods were combined in a single structure. Verandas or front porches with balustrades and soffit grilles were frequently used, and decorative details included perforated ornaments in the apex of the gable, filigree-like scrollwork on porches, and conical towers, usually placed to one side of the house rather than in the center as was so frequently seen in the Franco-American style.

Since there were apparently many houses of the Neo-Jacobean style

---

[28] Peat, *op. cit.*, pp. 149-150.

in Iowa City, only those which were outstanding or unusual examples of the style in their time and which have retained those characteristics are included. Three exceptions were made since pictures of those houses before remodeling or razing were available.

Houses With Towers

THE LINDSAY-LAKE HOUSE

Perhaps the most elaborate of the Neo-Jacobean houses remaining in Iowa City is the Lindsay-Lake house (Illustration 64), now converted into apartments. Built in 1893, the house is said to have been built from a set of standard plans which were sold by a Chicago firm of architects for $5.00. Today it is owned by Edith E. Lake.

The building combines exterior wall surfaces of siding, shingles of fish-scale shape, brick, and stone. The use of shingles to cover large

Illustration 64
The Lindsay-Lake House
935 East College Street
Photographed May 11, 1939 Courtesy, Fred W. Kent

areas as in the Ransom-Lake house did not occur in Indiana houses until the 1890's, according to Peat; before that time they were most frequently used to face the gable.

The foundation is of rough ashlar limestone with a water table of dressed rock. In the area beneath the large arched window and the chimney stack the stone treatment extends above the water table to the sill level. Dressed stone is used to form a window frame which flares outward at the top and bottom of the stiles and combines alternating voussoirs of light and dark colored stone with a keystone as its cap. Resting upon the keystone is a horizontal stone slab which in turn supports the stone sill of a rectangular window on the second floor. Thus stone work extends from the ground level to a point above the first-floor ceiling. The arch of the first-floor window is filled with stained lead glass in a sunflower pattern, a feature often found in houses of the 1890's.

The chimney stack is massive and forms the entire corner at the right of the facade, beginning above the water table and, in its original form, extending considerably above the roof line. Several feet of the decorative brick cap of the chimney have been removed. The lower part of the chimney has a corner buttress, an unusual English medieval feature, that terminates in a stone heading in which is a recessed trefoil type of pattern. Above the buttress and to the left near the rectangular window on the second floor is a decorative panel of circular forms carved from the brick. Above this and parallel with the top of the window the chimney tapers upward in a "skew table" formed of triangular-shaped dressed stones.

The main entrance to the house is at the left corner of the facade and has two approaches, one from each street. A veranda covers the area and extends an equal distance along the facade and the left side of the house. The balustrade is composed of spindles, and the posts are slender and round with arched supports beneath the entablature. In the central area is a frieze of spindles below a plain cornice which supports a shallow "candle-snuffer" tower with a finial. Behind this is a tall octagonal tower faced with fish-scale shingles on the second floor and with siding broken by round windows with diamond-shaped panes on the third floor. The roof of the tower is also eight-sided and is topped by a cast-iron finial. A similar cresting terminated the main roof line, and there was an iron decoration in the fleur-de-lis pattern placed on the stone sill beneath the rectangular window on the second floor adjacent to the chimney. The last two ornaments have been removed but are visible in a 1939 picture.

Other features of the facade are the second-floor porch with arched openings, short column supports, and balustrade of spindles and the large unperforated gable ornament composed of trefoil and sunburst designs. This gable also has bargeboards decorated with scallops and rosettes. Two gables on the right side of the house have perforated ornaments incorporating a half-wheel design.

On the right side of the house on the second floor is an oriel window abutting the chimney. Also on the right side is a one-story semipolygonal bay window on the first floor which has small curved brackets under the eaves and a roof that is curved in shape. On either side of its windows and below them as well are square wood panels cut in a shallow pyramidal shape.

On the left side before the house was remodeled the gable roof over a projecting area had a jerkin-head, according to a picture in the Kent files. There also was a perforated bargeboard below the eaves and a shallow rectangular bay with four large brackets giving visual support. To the rear of the left side was a small porch.

THE HAMMOND-HILLEL FOUNDATION HOUSE

All but unrecognizable due to extensive remodelings is the former residence of Miss Juliet M. Hammond, daughter of the first Dean of the Law College at the University, and now the headquarters for the Hillel Foundation (Illustration 65). The house was constructed in 1880 and had thirteen rooms.

In its original state the house was built mostly of siding with evidence of use of the psuedo half-timber technique on the two-story bay area which appears at the right in Illustration 65 and in the tower. Shingles were used only in the main gable and as a band of decoration on the tower above the main eave line of adjacent areas. The tower is octagonal and has rectangular windows on five sides on both the first and second floors. In the area over the roof line half-timbering forms horizontal panels. The roof of the tower is angular and cone-shaped and had a cast iron finial at its conclusion. The veranda, which has been removed, extended across the front and around on the right side to the projecting wing. Its decorative details included a balustrade of spindles, slender turned posts, an arched soffit grille with a minutely pierced edging, and a shallow balustrade on the roof with wood knobs forming finials at points directly above the posts.

The gable ornament formed, in effect, a screen in front of the shingled wall surface and the large round-arched window with its square panes.

Illustration 65
The Hammond-Hillel Foundation House
122 East Market Street
Photographed circa 1947 Courtesy, Fred W. Kent

Illustration 66
The Musser-Dixon House
715 East College Street
Photographed circa 1914 Courtesy, Fred W. Kent

Supported by two thin turned posts which rested on a balustrade was a triangular ornament in the peak of the gable which had an applied vine and leaf design. At the outer extremities of the gable as conclusions of the balustrade were triangular sunburst patterns.

The roof over the central portion of the building was a steeply-pitched hipped one with those on the wings being gabled. The one over the two-story bay on the right side of the house has a jerkin-head.

THE MUSSER-DIXON HOUSE

The Musser-Dixon house (Illustration 66) was the home of the William Musser family from the time it was built in 1890 until purchased by Professor James A. Dixon in 1963. According to the 1898 *Commercial Magazine*, Musser, a native of Iowa City, was ". . . the proprietor of the most complete lumber yard west of the Mississippi River, where you will find all kinds of lumber, hard or soft, white or black . . ."

As befitted a lumberman, the house was constructed of siding with some half-timbering, particularly in the tower. Bands of fish-scale shingles were placed on the facade at the level of the third floor, extending completely across the tower and the main block of the house, and on the projecting side wings between the first and second floors.

The porch which spans the front and part of the left side has a large sunburst design forming a rounded pediment over the front entrance and an elaborate balustrade divided into two registers and employing short bulbous spindles. The slender turned posts have jig saw brackets under a band of turned wood spindles which form the grille. The tower rises from the porch roof, is octagonal in shape, and in the third-floor area has an open porch with a semi-circular arched arcade. Small rosettes are applied on the spandrels of the arches. The roof is cone-shaped and terminates in a slender cast-iron finial.

The main roof combines hipped and gabled forms and features crest tiles at the apex of each roof line with voluted hip knobs at peripheral points. The carriage house at the rear of the property repeats this roof treatment and also has sunburst designs in the peaks of the two gables facing the street.

Instead of an ornament in the front gable a jerkin-head roof covers the apex. In contrast, both of the gable peaks on the side wings have applied vine and leaf ornaments above broad overhangs. The tall brick chimneys are large and feature offsets with decorative brick-work.

THE SUEPPEL-TAYLOR HOUSE

Another house which has been remodeled but retains most of its Neo-Jacobean decorative features is the Sueppel-Taylor house (Illustration 67) which was built in 1876. It is listed in county records as the property of Catherine Sueppel at that time and now is owned by J. Lee Taylor.

Outstanding Neo-Jacobean characteristics of the house are the veranda with turned posts and curved perforated grille under the cornice, the three-story octagonal tower on the right side of the house, and the elaborate gable ornament which combines turned spindles, scrolled brackets, and a perforated vine design. A picture in Aurner's history shows that on the right side of the house the veranda extended as far as the tower and at the corner of the facade had a short octagonal tower or pergola with round-arched openings and posts treated identically to those on the remainder of the porch. The same picture also shows that there were elaborate cast iron finials at the peak of every gable and tower, two of which remain. An unusual treatment is seen

Illustration 67
The Sueppel-Taylor House
425 East Jefferson Street

above the second-floor windows of the facade where the cornice across the gable combines two sections, one composed of beveled rectangles and the other a plain board cut at the bottom to suggest drapery swags. This rests directly on the lintels of three windows, each of which has a keystone design in the center which fits into the curve of the swags. The house employs the use of siding, shingles, and the false half-timber technique.

THE EICHER HOUSE

The residence of Mr. and Mrs. Frank Eicher, 1036 Woodlawn Avenue (Illustration 68), was built in 1893. The porch which extends across the facade has a rounded corner at the left side and above this is a round tower two-and-one-half stories high which terminates with a cone-shaped roof. The tower is open on the second floor level and has eyebrow windows in the half-story area. All of the porch and tower openings have slender turned posts and balustrades and grilles of turned spindles. The decoration in the apex of the facade gable is set into a projecting double gable which forms a roof for a small suspended balcony in front of the third-floor windows. This in turn provides a cover for a second-floor balcony which rests upon the

Illustration 68
The Eicher House
1036 Woodlawn Avenue

roof of the veranda. Filling the quarter circle between the third-floor balcony and the slanting roof line are large sunburst designs. The bargeboards over the balcony have alternating round and oval panels; the latter panels have incised Latin cross designs cut into them. The main bargeboard of the gable is composed of applied alternating circular and rectangular forms. On the left side of the house is a two-story semipolygonal bay window and adjacent to it is a rectangular half-timbered area surrounding a large sunburst design of wood.

THE MICHAEL-REDMAN HOUSE

Mrs. Aletha B. Redman's house (Illustration 69) was constructed in 1890 by Joseph Michael and has a three-story octagonal tower as its outstanding Neo-Jacobean feature. The tower roof is of the "candle-snuffer" type and at the level of the main gable of the house is surrounded by a pent roof. The porch which extends across the facade and back on both sides of the house has a balustrade and a grille of turned spindles, and each of the turned posts has two triangular scrolled brackets under the soffit grille. Next door at 308 East Church Street is the former home of Professor William A. Willis, who served as superintendent of Iowa City schools from 1884-1891 and later was principal of the Iowa City Academy. This house has had the veranda and cone of the tower removed, but otherwise it appears to have been all but identical to Mrs. Redman's house. A picture in Aurner's history confirms this.

THE MAIN-KAPPA SIGMA HOUSE AND THE WASHBURN HOUSE

Two additional houses of the Neo-Jacobean style with towers are not standing today, but both had distinctive characteristics of the English style. The Main-Kappa Sigma fraternity house (Illustration 70) was constructed of siding and featured half-timbering, a round open tower with a rounded outward-flaring roof which was placed on a square flat roof at the second-floor level, a large arch in the front gable in which was recessed a pair of rectangular windows and in front of which was a balcony which extended onto a projection of the house at the left of the facade, and a round porch at the left corner of the facade. The tower, the balcony, and the round porch had balustrades composed of thin turned spindles above which were goose-neck railings. The house also had an elaborate gable ornament composed of shingles and a design applied within a shallow triangular pediment, a large round-arched window on the first floor which incorporated a

Illustration 69
The Michael-Redman House
314 East Church Street

Illustration 70
The Main-Kappa Sigma House (Non-Extant)
932 East College Street
Photograph not dated Courtesy, Fred W. Kent

sunburst pattern of glass in the arch, and four small square windows with diamond-shaped panes on the second floor in the tower area. The house was built in 1895 for W. F. Main who was a manufacturing jeweler. A newspaper item of that year states that the house was designed and built by Louis E. Lyon and that, except for the necessity "to import a decorator" from Des Moines, it was entirely an Iowa City product.

Also non-extant is the former residence of Benson Earl Washburn (Illustration 71). Dr. Washburn and his wife, Evelyn Sinclair Washburn, were both osteopathic physicians. Their house represents the only known use in Iowa City of an onion dome, a form which became popular late in the nineteenth century through influence from Middle Eastern countries. Neo-Jacobean characteristics include the perforated gable ornaments with round-arched openings, the shingled gable areas, and the veranda with its balustrade and grille of turned spindles.

Houses Without Towers

THE HOUSER-BAUER HOUSE

Although stripped of its Neo-Jacobean decorative features, the former David L. Houser residence (Illustration 72) was photographed before it was remodeled and thus a record exists of a prime example of the style in Iowa City. The house was built in 1893 for Houser, a corn and coal dealer, who was regarded as one of the community leaders. *The Commercial Magazine* gave the following description of his activities and home:

Since coming to Iowa City ten years ago, Mr. Houser has been an active man in the welfare of the city. He has erected several complete, modern improved dwelling-houses, and his own home, which he erected regardless of cost, is located on the northwest corner of Iowa Avenue and Van Buren Street, on a beautiful high lot, 100 x 150 feet, with a spacious lawn, which is decorated with many rare and beautiful flowers, for which we must give full credit to Mrs. Houser for the artistic ideas and the grand arrangements of the same.[29]

Today the structure houses apartments and is owned by Fred T. Bauer.

The house is constructed of siding with several areas still showing the use of the favored half-timber technique. The Neo-Jacobean characteristic of beveling structural corners may be seen in the facade on the first floor of the entrance area and directly above this on the

---

[29] "Iowa City, Iowa," *The Commercial Magazine,* Vol. 1, No. 1 (January 1898), p. 42.

Illustration 71
The Washburn House (Non-Extant)
102 South Linn Street
Photograph from Aurner, *Leading Events in Johnson County, Iowa, History,* Vol.
2, page 729

Illustration 72
The Houser-Bauer House
430 Iowa Avenue
Photographed circa 1920 Courtesy, Fred W. Kent

second-floor balcony as well as on the projecting wing of the right side of the house.

In the 1951 remodeling the rounded front porch, the second-floor balcony, and a rear porch were removed, as well as ornaments in the front dormer and gable and the fleur-de-lis finials at the conclusion of the central hipped roof. The front porch had an elaborate lattice work balustrade which had round knobs centered in the vertical rails, a grille composed of solid areas cut with an elongated "X" design and open areas with short spindles, and turned posts with jig saw brackets at the top. Over the porch entrance was a projecting triangular pediment which was filled with an intricate scroll and leaf design in the center of which was the initial "H," in recognition of the family name. The second floor balcony rested upon the roof of the porch and had a short balustrade and four slender posts which appeared to support its roof which was formed by a projection of the gable above. A band of squares formed by half-timbering, a round-arched window, and an ornament with three spindles in its opening were the main decorative components of the gable. There was a plain bargeboard which was curved at the ends and near the apex of the gable, and the triangular areas on either side of the window had a diagonally striated pattern. The dormer window had fish-scale shingles on either side and was set behind a partial screen which had a large circular opening. The corners of the screen had elaborate perforated vine designs and around the area on all four sides was a band of perforated circles. In the peak of the dormer gable was an applied rosette with a leaf design on either side.

The fenestration of the entrance projection was completely changed from the original. A pair of standard rectangular windows were substituted for the door and round oculus window on the second floor, and the gable area was completely enclosed. In place of the large porch is a projecting gabled entrance with supporting columns.

THE FOSTER-HOCKEY HOUSE

A complicated roof contour which combines gable, hipped, and jerkin-head forms as well as dormer windows is seen on the Foster-Hockey apartment house (Illustration 73). Although many of its Neo-Jacobean characteristics have been removed in remodeling, the original roof form and several other identifying features remain. Instead of allowing the central hipped roof to rise to its usual conclusion, two gable peaks were introduced, adding to the irregularity of the overall composition. One of these gable peaks has a short pointed-

Illustration 73
The Foster-Hockey House
431 East Jefferson Street
Photograph not dated Courtesy, Fred W. Kent

arch window, the other a triangular window repeating the gable form. A part of the roof over a dormer window on the left side shows in the illustration as does the jerkin-head on the right side.

Also indicative of the original style is the two-story bay window set into the angle at the right of the facade. It is topped by a gable in which is a semi-circular window with square panes. Below this is a slanting cornice with an applied scrolled design. At the second-floor level were bands of shingles and rectangles formed by paneling; today these are covered by a finish of wide shingling which is applied to the entire exterior of the house. The porch with its curved soffit grille of spindles and its triangular pediment with a scrolled pattern has been removed, and the pedimented triple windows at the left of the bay were replaced by a horizontal single-paned modern one. The paired windows with a round-arched heading to the right of the bay area have also been replaced.

According to a newspaper article of the time, the house was constructed in 1894 by W. E. C. Foster at a cost of between $2,000 and $3,000. Foster held the property until 1939, and after that it served as chapter house for both the Kappa Kappa Gamma and the Zeta

Tau Alpha sororities before becoming an apartment house which is owned by Walter Hockey.

THE A. E. SWISHER HOUSE

The house formerly at 305 South Summit Street (Illustration 74) was erected for Abram E. Swisher, an attorney and president of the Citizen's Savings and Trust Company, by Sheets and Freyder, a firm of architects, contractors, and builders. A newspaper article dated August 12, 1896, reported the house as "nearing completion." In recent years it was the location of the Montessori School, but in 1966 it was razed to provide the site of a new home for the Delta Gamma sorority.

Three features of the house, the extensive use of dentils on the porch cornice and pediment and of round supporting columns and the broad plain cornice, suggest classic influence, but the overall stylistic impression was that of the Neo-Jacobean. Notable in this respect were the rounded porch which dominated the facade and sides, the two balconies on the second floor, the combination of gable and hip roof forms, and the treatment of the two-story bay area.

In addition to the previously-mentioned classic characteristics, the porch had a balustrade of turned spindles with a goose-neck railing, and in the triangular pediment over the entrance was an elaborate applied scroll design. One of the balconies was covered by the central hipped roof which was given visual support by two columns and a pilaster and had a balustrade and a soffit grille of spindles which suggested the form of a toy top. The other balcony was set under a gable projection at one side of the hipped roof and had no posts but had a balustrade which repeated that on the main porch in form and a bracket incorporating unusually thin spindles under the broad cornice.

All windows and doors on the first floor had segmental headings with simple undecorated lintels. Those on the second floor were round-arched and had headings that were chamfered and projecting. At either side of the second-floor windows in the bay were scrolled brackets which united to form a small pendant over the windows on the beveled sides. Above these was the main cornice under a broadly projecting flat roof, and on top of this and set into the gable was a short railing in front of a small window. The house was constructed of siding with some use of half-timbering and an almost unnoticed application of angular shingles between the balcony at the right and the porch roof.

Eight additional houses of wood construction are illustrative of the

Illustration 74
The A. E. Swisher House (Non-Extant)
305 South Summit Street Photographed in 1965

Neo-Jacobean style without towers and are worthy of study. They are the remodeled apartment house at 522 North Linn Street, owned by Frederick F. Drumm and Donna F. Jones and built in 1892 by Moses Bloom; the Regan-Oehler house, 922 East College Street, constructed in 1893; three 1888 houses, the Ranck-Davis-Sapp house, 230 South Dodge Street, the Wylie house, 1047 Woodlawn Avenue, and the Hicks house, 1011 Woodlawn Avenue; the Donahoe-Swisher-Woods house, 419 South Summit Street, 1883; the Guzeman-Olson house, 1224 Woodlawn Avenue, 1885; and the Sheets-Yakish house, 504 South Johnson Street, 1898 or shortly before. The latter house was constructed for J. M. Sheets of the Sheets and Freyder architectural and building firm.

Three brick houses without towers add to the wealth of examples of the Neo-Jacobean style.

THE PAINE-PENNINGROTH HOUSE

The Penningroth apartment house (Illustration 75) has been remodeled from a house constructed for Eugene Paine, a coal dealer. The date for the house is not clear; 1893 is cut into the heading above the large three-section front window, but county records state that the house was built in 1883. Pictured here before it was altered, the house shows strong resemblance to several Indiana houses which Peat classifies as Neo-Jacobean. The original square porch has been removed and the truncated Palladian window in the front gable has been replaced by a pair of rectangular windows. A variety of window treatments exist. The headings are heavy and combine brick and stone voussoirs with a stone keystone. The central window on the second floor has a heading which combines a carved stone cap and a heading of brick voussoirs which partially covers the wood lintel. The terminal stone voussoirs vary in shape from those on the other windows by having an outward projection suggesting a Dutch cap form. The first floor window is a triple one and combines a carved stone cap with a broad stone heading which curves to show the wood lintel but is straight at its top. This heading extends almost the width of the wall surface and has an incised decoration as well as a small keystone.

The corners of the projecting block of the Paine-Penningroth building are chamfered, suggesting a bay window form, and the gable roof of this area projects beyond the corners. Large solid triangular wooden brackets with small pendants form a transitional line between the roof and the walls. Above the entrance on the second floor is a slightly recessed rectangular panel of brick which is laid to form a checkerboard pattern. It has a flat dressed stone lintel and stone sill with the bricks below the sill set corner-wise to form a projection.

THE VOGT-UNASH HOUSE

Located high on a hill in the north part of town and facing the length of Van Buren Street, the brick house belonging to Miss Florence Unash (Illustration 76) was built in 1889 by her grandfather, Charles Vogt, at a cost of $5,000. It, too, is similar to Indiana houses of the style in its use of a dressed stone band or stringcourse a short distance below the tops of the second-floor windows, in the combined roof forms which include a small round dormer, and in the overall solid massiveness of the house. The porch has a round section suggesting a pergola at the left with a ribbed conical roof, and the entrance is formed by a large round arch that has spandrels formed by a square lattice pattern which is set diagonally in its frame. The area at the right of the entrance has a flat-arched soffit grille, and the balustrade is wood paneled and has no openings. The form of the flat-arched grille is repeated by the large first-floor window behind it which is divided into three sections by two vertical mullions. A

Illustration 75
The Paine-Penningroth House
530 South Clinton Street
Photographed circa 1947 Courtesy, Fred W. Kent

Illustration 76
The Vogt-Unash House
800 North Van Buren Street

panel of stained glass fills the top portion of the center section of this window. Other windows of the house are flat-arched with those on the second floor above the entrance having a dressed stone lintel with a carved shield forming a keystone.

THE RUPPERT HOUSE

The Ruppert house (Illustration 77) is built into the curve of a hill, thus revealing three stories on the facade and two to the rear. The facade is dominated by a two-story veranda which extends across two-thirds of the front. The veranda has slender turned posts on both levels and on the second floor has a balustrade of turned spindles and a grille of geometric lattice work. A gable which projects at right angles from the main gable forms a roof for the porch. The triangular part of this gable has two large rectangular windows, and the wall surface is covered by fish-scale shingles. The house was erected in 1884 as a farmhouse, well beyond the city limits.

Illustration 77
The Ruppert House
603 West Benton Street

HOUSES OF COMPOSITE OR ECLECTIC STYLE

Many of the foregoing houses employ characteristics associated with more than one style, but in each instance one style dominated the character of the house and permitted it to be classified. The following six houses which have been termed "Composite" or "Eclectic" combine features of two or more styles to such extent that no one style can be considered to be dominant.

THE PRATT-SOPER AND THE LEONARD-KOOL HOUSES

Two houses constructed in the mid-1880's combine characteristics of the Greek Revival and the Anglo-Italian styles. They are the Robert Soper residence (Illustration 78) and the Cornelius A. Kool house (Illustration 79). The Soper house was erected in 1885 by A. W. Pratt and the Kool house in 1883 by N. R. Leonard.

The main block of the Soper house is essentially Anglo-Italian, but the porch is mainly Greek Revival. However, this porch was an addition to the original structure before 1900 and thus is a part of the house as it was in the late nineteenth century. Each of the round fluted wood columns has an Ionic capital and an entasis, and the cornice has an entablature which is undecorated except for the frieze of dentils. The porch balustrade does not have the lightness and delicacy of those of the Neo-Jacobean style; rather, it uses heavier vase-shaped balusters below a goose-neck railing. Anglo-Italian characteristics include brick window headings with single keystones of dressed rock, round oculus windows in gables each with four keystones, and large coupled brackets against the broad cornice under the eaves. All of the second-floor windows are round-arched, and those on the first-floor facade are segmental-arched. The house has had several additions according to real estate records, and among them was the one void of openings at the right of the porch. Originally, it housed the pipes for a pipe organ. This part has recently been remodeled.

The Kool house also has a Greek Revival porch which has a broadly overhanging gable roof with a shallow triangular pediment. The lower part of the shaft of the round fluted wood columns has been left plain. The doorway treatment combines pilasters which repeat the details of the columns with side lights and a transom. The crowding of the windows on either side of the porch suggests that the porch was an addition, but no factual information has been found to support this assumption. Familiar Italianate features such as single and coupled brackets, an oval gable window, and a one-story bay

Illustration 78
The Pratt-Soper House
503 Melrose Avenue

Illustration 79
The Leonard-Kool House
226 South Johnson Street

window at one end of the house are present. The second-floor windows have segmental headings, and those on the first floor are rectangular with a flat heading.

THE SLEZAK-HUBBARD HOUSE

One of the few nineteenth century houses in Iowa City which can be documented as being designed by an architect is the former Joseph Slezak house (Illustration 80). The tan brick house was constructed in 1892 with O. H. Carpenter the architect and J. J. Hotz the contractor, according to the 1898 *Commercial Magazine.* Today the house is owned by William C. Hubbard and has been remodeled into apartments.

The house is an amazing amalgamation of details and suggests that the designer's imagination was allowed to run the gamut of architectural ideas. The roof combines gables with a hipped form, but there its resemblance to the Neo-Jacobean prototype ends. The gable overhangs are practically non-existent, and the gable slopes end with elaborate inward scrolls. Bargeboards are formed by stairstep-shaped boards, and small but intricate applied ornaments fill the gable peaks.

Illustration 80
The Slezak-Hubbard House
328 Brown Street
Photographed circa 1920 Courtesy, Fred W. Kent

The gable on the left side of the house has a large round window which is divided vertically by two mullions; the front gable and the one on the right side have two round-arched windows with dressed rock keystones. On the roof above the two-story polygonal bay window at the left corner of the facade was a wood balustrade with round finials topping the main posts. In shape this balustrade conformed to the bay beneath, but it had no function other than a decorative one, and there was no access to the roof area behind it. This feature has been removed.

Except for the area under the front gable, a broad cornice that has a wide frieze composed of formal classic garlands and wreaths encircles the entire house. This cornice rests directly upon the second-floor windows. The first-floor windows are segmentally arched and have brick voussoirs between terminal voussoirs and a keystone of dressed rock. On the left side of the house serving a stairwell is a large round-arched window with elaborate stained glass patterns in both its arched and rectangular panes. Also on the left side is a two-story bay which formerly was topped by a balustrade with posts which had pointed finials. Again the balustrade's function was decorative for the only access to the area it confined was through the round window behind it.

The porch which is at the left of the facade originally had triple round columns which sprang from a square paneled base, a balustrade of spindles, and a cornice with a frieze of dentils. Today there are single round columns at the corners and no balustrade.

The house is set upon a high base of semi-dressed ashlar stone and has a water table of dressed rock. The carriage house at the rear of the property was a part of the complete architectural composition and used red brick, segmental arched headings for the openings, voussoirs of brick, and horizontal boarding in the gables.

THE OVERHOLT-PLUM HOUSE

Built in 1873 by Henry D. Overholt, the one-and-one half story house owned by Jerry L. Plum (Illustration 81) combines characteristics that are Colonial, Greek Revival, and Victorian in origin.

Each of the heavy brick end walls which extends above the line of the gable roof, is stepped, and incorporates two chimney shafts, has influence that may be recognized as Dutch or Flemish Colonial. The broad porch or one-story portico is classic in origin with its round unfluted columns, plain cornice, and triangular pediment. The face of this shallow pediment is filled with rows of fish-scale shingles, a feature which appeared with the Neo-Jacobean style. The porch roof and the main roof are separated by a broad plain classic cornice which has the basic elements of a complete entablature but lacks its decorative detail. The entrance projects onto the porch and is beveled at the corners.

The roof is broken by a central gable which repeats the form of the porch pediment but is much larger in scale. The wall surface of this gable is boarded horizontally and has a small vertical sash window with a simple flat lintel. On either side of the gable are two large dormers which have jerkin-head roofs.

On the right end of the house is a one-story frame bay window, a feature which appears in several of the Victorian styles. This is half-timbered or paneled in the Neo-Jacobean style. The cornice of the bay is simple and classic in style.

Illustration 81
The Overholt-Plum House
726 Iowa Avenue

THE ANTON LINDER HOUSE

Located just north of the city limits, the rural residence of the John
S. Way family (Illustration 82) is identified with an early Iowa City
settler, Anton Linder. He came to the area in 1850 and originally
lived in a log cabin and homesteaded the land for this house. Linder
and his wife actually constructed the house themselves circa 1860,
even digging the clay and firing the bricks on the site. A depression
exists north of the house and is thought to be the location of the
clay source and the kiln. The brick part of the house is a rectangular
block with the entrance at the right in the gable end. Except for
the porch which is similar to many of those on houses of the Neo-
Jacobean style, the house is similar to the group of houses in the
Greek Revival section which feature entrances in gable ends.

THE MACBRIDE-PICKERING HOUSE

Iowa City has many houses which were constructed near the end of
the nineteenth century which have the gambrel roof form. The origin
of this double-pitched roof is not clear, but Morrison considers that
there are several different interpretations of the gambrel which probably had equally as many sources, England, the Flemish area of
southern Holland, western Belgium, and northern France, Sweden,
and Germany.[30] The gambrel roof of the James N. Pickering house
(Illustration 83) has a very narrow upper slope and a very deep
lower slope, suggesting possible English or New England ancestry.
The frame house also features an octagonal castellated tower, a
medieval characteristic, which is covered by a band of fish-scale
shingles at its conclusion. The house also has a narrow overhang at
the division of the first and second floors, an entrance porch with a
balustrade of spindles and small wood columns with scrolled Ionic
capitals above stone piers, and an oriel window on the left side of
the first floor. The house was constructed in 1893 on property owned
by Thomas H. Macbride who served The University of Iowa as a
distinguished botanist for many years and as president from 1914 to
1916.

Additional houses in Iowa City which are eclectic in style could be
cited. One of the more interesting is the red brick house of Arthur
D. Vosburg, 1029 North Dodge Street, which was constructed in 1896.

---

[30] Hugh Morrison, *Early American Architecture* (New York: Oxford University Press, 1952), pp. 37, 123, and 506.

Illustration 82
The Anton Linder House
Linder Road

Illustration 83
The Macbride-Pickering House
17 South Governor Street
Photographed circa 1920 Courtesy, Fred W. Kent

CHAPTER 4

TWO HISTORIC
IOWA CITY CHURCHES

Although the main focus of this study has been upon architectural styles of nineteenth century houses in Iowa City, two churches built within the 1839-1900 time limitation exemplify an ecclesiastical interpretation of two of the major styles discussed.

Previously cited as an example of the only extant use of boards and battens in the Gothic Revival style, Trinity Episcopal Church (Illustration 84) has additional features of the style. Among them are the pointed arch conclusions of the vertical battens on the facade, the many pointed arch windows, and the large trefoil exterior decorations in wood on either side. The following quotation is significant in assessing the design of the church:

On January 16th, 1871, the plan of the Church was selected, being a modification of one of [Richard] Upjohn's plans for Gothic Churches; and on the 23rd of the same month a contract was approved for its erection (by Mr. Sheets) at a cost of $6,250.[1]

The oldest church in Iowa City, the First Presbyterian Church (Illustration 85), was begun in 1856 following a fire which had destroyed the earlier one and was completed in 1865. The original spire was blown off during a storm in 1877 and was replaced by the present square castellated tower. The structure has many characteristics of Italian influence including the arched windows with heavy decorative caps, the coupled windows in the tower, the projecting entrance pavilion, and the three fringe-like decorations produced by variations in the laying of the brick in the pavilion area.

---

[1] Samuel N. Watson, *History of Trinity Parish*. A Sermon Delivered in Trinity Church, Iowa City, Iowa, April 9, 1893, and Printed by Request.

Illustration 84
Trinity Episcopal Church
College and Gilbert Streets
Photograph not dated Courtesy, Fred W. Kent

Illustration 85
First Presbyterian Church
Market and Clinton Streets
Photograph not dated Courtesy, Fred W. Kent

APPENDIX

To aid the reader, the following terms are included through the courtesy of John Wiley & Sons, Inc., New York, from their publication, *Dictionary of Architecture*, by Henry H. Saylor. Except as noted, all definitions are from this source.

ARCHITRAVE: in classic architecture, the member of an entablature resting on the capitals of columns or piers and supporting the frieze.

ASHLAR: masonry having a face of square or rectangular stones.

BARGEBOARD (VERGEBOARD): the vertical-face board following and set back under, the roof edge of a gable, sometimes decorated by carving.

BELVEDERE: an open pavilion built for a view, either on top of a building or as an independent building.

BRACKET: a supporting member for a projecting floor or shelf, sometimes in the shape of an inverted L and sometimes as a solid piece or a triangular truss.

BRACKET CAPITAL: a capital having bracket forms projecting as a continuing support of the lintel.

CAPITAL: the top member or group of members of a column, pier, shaft, or pilaster.

CASTELLATED: bearing turrets or battlements, like a fortified castle.

CHAMFER: to cut away the edge where two surfaces meet in an exterior angle, leaving a bevel at the junction.

CORBEL: a bracket form, usually produced by extending successive courses of masonry or wood beyond the wall surface.

CORONA: the flat vertical member of a classical cornice between the cymatium above and the bed molding below.

CREST OR CRESTING: a decorative ridge for a roof, usually as a continuous series of finials.

DENTIL: one of a series of block-like projections forming a molding.

ENTABLATURE: in classical architecture, the horizontal group of members immediately above the column capitals; divided into three major parts, it consists of architrave, frieze, and cornice.

ENTASIS: the subtle curve by which the shaft of a column is diminished in section above the cylindrical lowest third.

FINIAL: a terminal form at the top of spire, gable, gatepost, pinnacle, or other point of relative hight.

FLAT ARCH: an arch whose intrados is a horizontal line.

GOOSE-NECK: a ramp of the handrail on a stair or railing.

GRILLE: a frame of bars, slender balusters, or other openwork, usually decorative, to serve as a screen.

HEADING: something that serves as a head, top, or front.[1]

HORSESHOE ARCH: an arch whose intrados includes more than a semicircle.

IMPOST: the cap of a pier or pilaster supporting the spring of an arch.

INTRADOS: the curved surface bounded by the parallel lower edges of an arch—its soffit.

JACOBEAN: designating the period of early seventeenth century in England.

JERKIN-HEAD: a roof form in which the top of a gable is cut off by a secondary slope forming a hip.

LANCET ARCH: a sharply pointed arch.

LINTEL: the horizontal member of the most common structural form —a beam resting its two ends upon separate posts.

MODILLION: a bracket form used in series under a corona.

MULLION: an upright division member between windows or doors in a close series.

OCULUS: a circular opening, occasionally formed at the top of a dome.

ORIEL: a projecting window with its walls corbeled or supported by brackets.

PEDIMENT: the triangular face of a roof gable, especially in its classical form.

PENDANT, OR PENDENT: an ornamental member suspended from above.

PENT ROOF: a roof of a single sloping plane.

PILASTER: an engaged pier of shallow depth; in classical architecture it follows the height and width of related columns, with similar base and cap.

PORTE-COCHERE: a shelter for vehicles outside an entrance doorway.

PORTICO: an entrance porch.

QUATREFOIL: a four-lobed figure in variations.

QUOIN: one of the corner stones of a wall when these are empha-

---

[1] Barnhart, C. L. (ed.). *The American College Dictionary* (New York: Random House, 1962), p. 557.

sized by size, by more formal cutting, by more conspicuous jointing, or by difference in texture.

RAIL: a horizontal member in a panel frame, as in a paneled door between the stiles. 2. the top member connecting the posts of a fence or a row of balusters.

RANDOM ASHLAR: masonry of square- or rectangular-face stones, with neither vertical nor horizontal joints continuous.

RUBBLE: broken, untrimmed stone used in masonry. Random rubble is masonry laid with no course lines, as the stone comes.

SEGMENTAL ARCH: a round arch whose intrados includes less than a semicircle.

SKEW TABLE: the stones forming the slopes of the offsets of buttresses and other projections.[2]

SOFFIT: the finished underside of a lintel, arch, or other spanning member, usually overhead.

SPANDREL: the surface at the side of a half-arch between a vertical line at the bottom of the archivolt and a horizontal line through its top.

STILE: a vertical framing member of a paneled door or of paneling.

STILTED ARCH: an arch in which the center is above the impost line.

STRINGCOURSE: a plain or molded horizontal continuous band on an exterior wall.

TYMPANUM: the space enclosed by the three molded sides of a pediment, or by the lines of a semicircular overdoor panel or the like.

VERGEBOARD: see bargeboard.

VOLUTE: a spiral ornament such as used as a pair in the Ionic capital.

VOUSSOIR: one of the stones of an arch lying between impost and keystone.

WATER TABLE: a projecting base course, beveled at the top for weathering.

---

[2] John Henry Parker, *A Concise Glossary of Architecture* (London and Oxford: Parker & Company, 1888), p. 257.

BIBLIOGRAPHY

Primary Sources

MANUSCRIPTS

Gilman Folsom Collection. [Personal letters and records]. (State Historical Society of Iowa, Iowa City).

Johnson County Copy of Original Entries [n.d., but considered to be prior to 1870]. (Johnson County Courthouse, Iowa City).

Johnson County Deed Records. 1839-1967. (Johnson County Courthouse, Iowa City).

Johnson County Transfer Book, Iowa City & Additions, No. 1 [n.d.].

Johnson County Transfer Book, Iowa City & Additions, No. 3 [n.d.].

Johnson County Transfer Book, Lands, Range 6, Books 1-2 [n.d.].

Miller, A. B. *Abstract of Original Deeds from the State of Iowa, for Lots in Iowa City, November 19, 1860.* (Johnson County Courthouse, Iowa City).

GOVERNMENT DOCUMENTS

Journal of the House of Representatives of the First Legislative Assembly of Iowa Territory. Burlington, Iowa: Clarke and McKenny, Printers, 1839.

Journal of the House of Representatives of the General Assembly of the State of Iowa. Burlington: The Hawk-Eye Office, 1847.

Journal of the House of Representatives of the Second Legislative Assembly of Iowa Territory. Burlington: J. Gardiner Edwards, 1840.

Journal of the House of Representatives of the State of Iowa. Iowa City: Mahony and Dorr, 1855.

Minot, George (ed.) *The Statutes at Large and Treaties of the United States of America.* Vol. 9. Boston: Little, Brown and Company, 1854.

Peters, Richard (ed.). *The Public Statutes at Large of the United States of America.* Vol. 5. Boston: Little, Brown and Company, 1856.

NEWSPAPERS

Iowa Capital Reporter, Dec. 11, 1841-June 3, 1846; 1859-1861.

Iowa City Citizen, 1893-1900.

Iowa City Daily Crescent, Aug.-Sept. 1857.

Iowa City Daily Reporter, May 28-Nov. 5, 1856.

Iowa City Herald, 1893-1897; Jan.-March 26, 1898.

Iowa City Journal, March 27, 1879-May 14, 1880.

Iowa City Press [Weekly], Feb. 1864-Dec. 1867; 1869; 1871; 1873-1900.

Iowa City Standard, 1840-1844; June 1846-June 7, 1848.

Iowa City Republican [Daily], Jan.-June 1884; 1885.

Iowa City Republican [Weekly], Nov. 1864-1869; Oct. 1875-1892; 1899.

Iowa State Democratic Press (includes *Iowa City Daily Press* and *State Press*) [Daily], Aug.-Dec. 1860; 1861-1900.

ATLASES, GAZETEERS, AND MAPS

Atlas of Johnson County, Iowa. Davenport, Iowa: The Huebinger Survey and Map Publishing Company, 1900.

Atlas of Johnson County, Iowa. Iowa City: J. J. Novak, 1889.

Bird's Eye View of Iowa City, Johnson County, Iowa [no publisher given], 1868.

Johnson County, Iowa, Atlas. Geneva, Illinois: Thompson and Everts, 1870.

Map of Iowa City. Drawn by L. [Leander] Judson, July 4, 1839. Recorded July 13, 1839, Plat Record 1, p. 116, Recorder's Office, Johnson County, Iowa [Retraced by S. S. Hovey, May 12, 1906].

Map of Iowa City, Johnson County, Iowa. Compiled and drawn by J. H. Millar, Bryan & Millar, Panora, Iowa. Illustrations by G. H. Yewel. Lithographed by W. Schuchman, Pittsburgh, Pennsylvania, 1854.

Newhall, John B. *Sketches of Iowa, or the Emigrant's Guide.* New York: J. H. Colton, 1841.

Parker, Nathan Howe. *Iowa As It Is in 1855; a Gazetteer for Citizens and a Hand-book for Emmigrants* [*sic*]. Chicago: Keen and Lee, 1855.

_____. *The Iowa Handbook for 1856.* Boston: John P. Jewett and Company, 1856.

BOOKS

Davis, Alexander Jackson. *Rural Residences.* New York: To Be Had of the Architect, at the New York University, and of booksellers generally, throughout the United States, c. 1837.

Downing, Andrew Jackson. *Cottage Residences.* New York: John Wiley, 1853.

_____. *The Architecture of Country Houses.* New York: D. Appleton and Company, 1850.

Fowler, Orson S. *A Home for All or the Gravel Wall and the Octagon Mode of Building.* New York: Fowler and Wells, 1854.

History of Johnson County, Iowa. Iowa City: [no author or publisher given], 1883.

Parker, John Henry. *A Concise Glossary of Architecture.* London and Oxford: Parker & Company, 1888.

Portrait and Biographical Record of Johnson, Poweshiek, and Iowa Counties, Iowa. Chicago: Chapman Brothers, 1893.

Tuttle, Charles R. *An Illustrated History of the State of Iowa.* Chicago: Richard S. Peale and Company, 1876.

Vaux, Calvert. *Villas and Cottages.* New York: Harper and Brothers, 1857.

Wheeler, Gervase. *Homes for the People.* New York: Charles Scribner, 1855.

PERIODICALS

"Iowa City, Iowa," *The Commercial Magazine,* Vol. 1, No. 1 (January, 1898).

Irish, F. [Frederick] M. "History of Johnson County, Iowa," *Annals of Iowa,* Vol. 6, No. 1 (January, 1868), pp. 23-31; No. 2 (April, 1868), pp. 105-120; No. 3 (July, 1868), pp. 191-215; No. 4 (October, 1868), pp. 302-328.

Negus, Charles. "The Early History of Iowa," *Annals of Iowa,* Vol. 7, No. 4 (October, 1869), pp. 317-326.

Sanders, Cyrus. "History of Johnson County, IV," *Early Iowa: the Iowa City Republican Leaflet,* No. 4 (October 6, 1880), pp. 15-16.

Secondary Sources

MANUSCRIPT

Data Sheets, Real Estate Appraisement, Johnson County, City of Iowa City, Ward 1, Books 1 and 2; Ward 2, Books 1 and 2; Ward 3 (complete); Ward 4, Books 1 and 2; Ward 5, Books 1 and 2 [c. 1940].

NEWSPAPERS

Des Moines Sunday Register, March 30, 1858.

Iowa City Press-Citizen, August 13, 1926; August 14, 1926; May 15, 1961; April 8, 1964.

The Daily Iowan, student newspaper, The University of Iowa; [n.d., unpaged].

BOOKS

Andrews, Wayne. *Architecture, Ambition and Americans.* New York: Harper and Brothers, 1955.

Aurner, Charles [Clarence] Ray. *Leading Events in Johnson County, Iowa, History.* Vol. 1: Historical, 1912; Vol. 2: Biographical, 1913. Cedar Rapids, Iowa: Western Historical Press.

Briggs, John Ely (ed.). *Cumulative Index to the Palimpsest,* Vols. 1-10 (1920-1929). Iowa City: The State Historical Society of Iowa, 1941.

Burchard, John E., and Bush-Brown, Albert. *The Architecture of America: A Social and Cultural History.* Boston: Little, Brown and Company, 1961.

Drury, John. *Historic Midwest Houses.* Minneapolis: The University of Minnesota Press, 1947.

_____. *Old Illinois Houses.* Springfield, Illinois: Illinois State Historical Society, 1948.

Eberlein, Harold D. *The Architecture of Colonial America.* Boston: Little, Brown and Company, 1921.

Federal Writers' Project. *Iowa, A Guide to the Hawkeye State.* New York: The Viking Press, 1938.

Fitch, James M. *American Building: The Forms That Shape It.* Boston: Houghton, Mifflin Company, 1948.

Frary, I. [Ihna] T. *Early Homes of Ohio.* Richmond, Virginia: Garrett and Massie, 1936.

Gallaher, Ruth A. (ed.). *Cumulative Index to the Palimpsest,* Vols. 11-21 (1930-1940). Iowa City: The State Historical Society of Iowa, 1942.

_____. *Iowa Journal of History and Politics Cumulative Index,* Vols. 1-40 (1903-1942). Iowa City: The State Historical Society of Iowa, 1944.

Giedion, Sigfried. *Space, Time and Architecture.* 3rd ed. enlarged. Cambridge: The Harvard University Press, 1954.

Gowans, Alan. *Images of American Living.* Philadelphia and New York: J. B. Lippincott Company, 1964.

Hamlin, Talbot. *Greek Revival Architecture in America.* London and New York: Oxford University Press, 1944.

Historic American Buildings Survey. Washington, D.C.: United States Government Printing Office, National Park Service, United States Department of the Interior, 1941.

Hitchcock, Henry-Russell. *Architecture: Nineteenth and Twentieth Centuries.* Baltimore: Penguin Books, 1958.

Kouwenhoven, John A. *Made In America: The Arts in Modern Civilization.* Garden City: Doubleday, 1948.

Maass,. John. *The Gingerbread Age: A View of Victorian America.* New York: Rinehart and Company, 1957.

Morrison, Hugh. *Early American Architecture.* New York: Oxford University Press, 1952.

Mumford, Lewis. *The Brown Decades.* New York: Harcourt, Brace and Company, 1931.

————. *Sticks and Stones.* New York: Horace Liveright, Publisher, 1924.

Newcomb, Rexford. *Architecture of the Old Northwest Territory.* Chicago: The University of Chicago Press, 1950.

Peat, Wilbur D. *Indiana Houses of the Nineteenth Century.* Indianapolis: Indiana Historical Society, 1962.

Perrin, Richard W. E. *Historic Wisconsin Buildings: A Survey of Pioneer Architecture 1835-1870.* Milwaukee: Milwaukee Public Museum, 1962.

Petersen, William J. *Iowa History Reference Guide.* Iowa City: The State Historical Society of Iowa, 1952.

Roos, Frank J., Jr. *Writings on Early American Architecture.* Columbus: The Ohio State University Press, 1943.

Saylor, Henry H. *Dictionary of Architecture.* New York: John Wiley & Sons, Inc., 1963.

Shambaugh, Benjamin F. *Iowa City: A Contribution to the Early History of Iowa.* Iowa City: The State Historical Society of Iowa, 1893.

————. *The Old Stone Capitol Remembers.* Iowa City: The State Historical Society of Iowa, 1939.

Williams, Henry Lionel, and Williams, Ottalie K. *A Guide to Old American Houses.* New York: A. S. Barnes and Company, Inc., 1962.

PERIODICALS

Ingram, Patricia Smith. "Hudson: Early Nineteenth Century Domestic Architecture," *Journal of the Society of Architectural Historians,* Vol. 12, No. 2 (May, 1953), pp. 9-14.

"Iowa City, Iowa, A City of Homes," Published by the Iowa City Commercial Club, 1914.

Lancaster, Clay. "Japanese Buildings in the United States Before 1900; Their Influence Upon American Domestic Architecture," *Art Bulletin,* Vol. 35 (September, 1953), pp. 217-224.

Petersen, William J. "Population Advance to the Upper Mississippi Valley 1830-1860," *The Iowa Journal of History and Politics,* Vol. 32, No. 3 (July, 1934), pp. 312-353.

Richman, Irving B. "John Brown's Band," *The Palimpsest,* Vol. 41, No. 1 (January, 1960), pp. 16-22.
Roos, Frank J., Jr. "Ohio: Architectural Crossroad," *Journal of the Society of Architectural Historians,* Vol. 12, No. 2 (May, 1953), pp. 3-8.
Springer, John. "Sylvanus Johnson," *Iowa Historical Record,* Vol. 18, No. 2 (April, 1902), pp. 449-456.
Swisher, Jacob A. "Plum Grove," *The Palimpsest,* Vol. 29, No. 1 (January, 1948), pp. 19-32.
"The House That Johnson Built," *Staff Magazine* (The University of Iowa), Vol. 3, No. 2 (November, 1952), pp. 3-9.

UNPUBLISHED MATERIAL

Cooper, Mabel R. "Nineteenth Century Home Architecture of Marshall, Michigan." Unpublished Doctoral Dissertation, Florida State University, 1963.
Ellis, Edwin Charles. "Certain Stylistic Trends in Architecture in Iowa City." Unpublished Master's Thesis, State University of Iowa, 1947.
Roos, Frank J., Jr. "An Investigation of the Sources of Early Architectural Design in Ohio." Unpublished Doctoral Dissertation, Ohio State University, 1937.
Van der Zee, Jacob (comp.). *Annals of Iowa Index* (1863-1909). Typescript [n.d.].
Watson, Samuel N. *History of Trinity Parish.* A Sermon Delivered in Trinity Church, Iowa City, Iowa, April 9, 1893, and Printed by Request.

INTERVIEWS WITH IOWA CITY RESIDENTS

Bristol, Mrs. Wm. Frank. May 5, 1964.
Carson, Mrs. George S., Sr. May 3, 1965.
Chudwick, Mrs. Walter C. April 3, 1965.
Copeland, Virgil S. October 15, 1965.
Green, Edwin B. May 3, 1965.
Gilmore, Mrs. Eugene. May 27, 1965.
Glasgow, Mrs. Bruce R. May 25, 1965.
Griffin, Mrs. Cora U. October 6, 1965.
Kelly, Mrs. Louise B. May 29, 1965.
Kent, Fred W. February 18, 1965.
Kent, Gordon. February 18, 1965.
Keyser, Clarence W. October 13, 1965.

Kuhl, Mr. and Mrs. Ernest P. March 26, 1965.
Lang, Mrs. Allen N. May 14, 1965.
Linder, Mr. and Mrs. Henry. May 26, 1965.
Louis, Norwood C., II. October 8, 1965.
Miltner, E. C. October 18, 1965.
Negus, Mrs. Lewis H. October 13, 1965.
Neuzil, Rev. Edward W. October 15, 1965.
Pownall, Mr. and Mrs. Fred M. May 7, 1964.
Rigler, Mrs. George Harold. May 2, 1965; February 11, 1967.
Scheuerman, Mrs. Milton [Sharm]. September 27, 1965.
Smith, Miss Lula E. March 19, 1965.
Soper, Mrs. Robert. October 22, 1965.
Stach, Miss May. May 22, 1965.
Swisher, Mrs. Scott. October 13, 1965.
Turner, Mr. and Mrs. Thomas S. April 20, 1964.
Wheeler, Mrs. Paul. May 3, 1965.

OTHER SOURCES

Cox, Thomas G. Lecture, Iowa City Recreation Center, Iowa City. April 21, 1965.
Rasmussen, Wayne D. Chief, Agricultural History Branch, United States Department of Agriculture, Washington, D.C. Letter, October 9, 1961.